Release Note

Release	Remarks
12 March '11 - Zeitgeist [illegible] Versi[illegible]	[illegible] [illegible]py) have been [illegible]nt in [illegible]
13 August [illegible] Landjuwe[illegible] Novaglob[illegible] symposium Amsterdam	[illegible] [illegible]onomy [illegible] [illegible]ation, Limited
September '11 Edition	• Input 13 August Novaglobe symposium processed, especially naming input of Daniel Roos (Novaglobe Conscious Council) and Johannes Heimrath (Club of Budapest) • Section added on immigrant problem solution (Togetherhood chapter). • Sections added on 12V standardisation and 'Keep idea free' foundation (Flowconomy chapter). • Daniel Roos / Iwanjka: propose to make a 'ring of music' around essence of goodness description (333 words). Sufi style. • Johannes Heimrath suggests 'Harmoniarchi' instead of the word 'Harmonicracy'. • Iwanjka proposes 'Transjustice' instead of 'Justitea'. • Some minor changes / additions, and total textual review. • Ready for publication via Amazon and www.boekenroute.nl

---Quotes ---

"We have the chance to turn the pages over"
[Song - John Farnham, You are the Voice]

"Worldshift is needed, fast."
The choice is yours: a quantum leap upwards or downwards
[Ervin Laszlo]

"The Survival of the Fittest has Ended,
The Revival of the Goodest has only just begun"
[Iwanjka]

"Yes, there are two paths you can go by
But in the long run
There's still time to change
The road you're on"
[Stairway to Heaven, Led Zeppelin]

"*Be* the change you wanna see"
[Mahathma Ghandi]

Author Iwanjka, Inspired by Many, www.iwanjka.com

ISBN 978-90-815775-4-0
NUR 740
Publisher: Deniesa

1 You may send the Ebook forward, but the reader is considered as though he/ she purchased the book (once reading further than this section). Please make a fair donation, the money is used for making the worldshift. See www.novaglobe.org → Reason, for pricing information. As soon as we have realised the change, we can hopefully abandon copyright issues...

Contents

1 Preface

This book is about global change. It is not a book about looking at all 'the bad things' in society. It is about looking at society and thinking: "Imagine I am the architect of a world, and I have a blank canvas, what would I be painting?". That is what I did. And than I discovered that actually we have the chance to make that new world. Why not?

I myself got jammed in life in 2008. I had been working for 10 years in the banking industry. A mortgage, housing market fears, the upcoming financial crisis, and not knowing how to address my energy resources made me crash. I saw the inner side of psychiatry, I experienced hell on earth. And now I want to create heaven on earth.

This book is about the quantum leap upwards. These are the words of Ervin Laszlo, not mine. This book is about doing it together. About our combined global consciousness, wisdom and power. About the 'ONE' thought, think of the same named song of U2.

I would like this book to be an open source book. I am the lucky one acting as the mediator. I am the person writing it down. But the ideas of many are in it. It is very well possible that in next editions new ideas, of people from all over the world who read it, will be included. ,thus putting our combined creativity to maximum expression. That is what I hope for and intendto do. So, everybody is invited and free to react...

"Eyes into the Promised Land" is a song I created about 2 years ago. It stands for the beautiful thing of eye contact and spontaneous love. It also stands for the change philosophy I believe in: do not focus on bad things, do not 'fight' the system, focus on creation instead. And befree the system (compassion value). Focus on the light. On the other hand it is necessary to understand present (sub) systems of our ecosystem in a profound manner to redesign them in a more sound fashion. And we should put effort in avoiding the 'bad' system to grow...

So, in this book, you will not find an elaborate analysis on why the present systems are not 'good' (anymore). On the Novaglobe website we collect -often existing- titles of various books and writers addressing these analyses.

In this book (Novaglobe) you'll find the outlines of the proposed redesign of primary eco-subsystems of our society. Again, the ideas of this redesign are based on inspiration of all cultures and all countries of this world. Thus making an new sound global chord...

The main addressed sub-eco systems are:

- The subsystem required for producing and exchanging goods and services including the money system, currntly called 'economy'. Novaglobe variant name: **Flowconomy**.
- The subsystem required for organising our society, currently called 'government and politics'. Novaglobe variant name: **Harmonicracy**.
- Other main subsystems like education, (mental) health care, religion, safety, global help, etc. will be addressed in their outlines as well. See part 'Design' for the various eco subdomains in Novaglobe.

The hope and intention is that in an open source and synchronous manner people start writing books on these various topics. That way,I can put pointers from this book to those books and create a complete, detailed plan for our new world. We could maintain these designs / plan in a central manner, with for instance a wiki. And that in each country, people can use it to their advantage . It will never become demanding, people are free to choose their way of living. Use it as a set of tools . Guidelines. Global collective inspiration.

About implementing it

Making a plan is one thing. Realising it is another. I spent10 years migration projects in the banking industry. The migration process for the 'current'-situation towards the 'desired state' is the most intriguing part. Therefore a substantial part of this book will be addressed to the 'migration plan'. The road map towards Novaglobe.

This migration path is not 'ready' yet. And in next editions of this book - the intention is to release a new edition every six months - ideas of fellow change makers, allied movements (political and non-political) will be included, of course giving them credit for it. And thus a coherent and evolving plan will be synthesised, which is already being implemented along the way.

Like a giant migration project...

Biarritz / Lanzarote / Amersfoort,

Second edition, August 2011

2 Introduction

August 2010. I am in Biarritz, a small city at the Atlantic Ocean in France. I left the Netherlands for about one and a half weeks to write a substantial part of a book which started to emerge some months earlier in my consciousness.A book bythe name "Deniesa's Manifest".

In the previous two years I had been occupied with writing a book on psychiatry ('Diagnosis Lifejam') and the sick elements of our society, and I had been occupied with the establishment of a Dutch new political party called 'New Netherlands'. I even had the honour to act as the 'campaign leader', in the run-up towards the 9th of June 2010 Dutch national elections. This resulted in 2133 voters. Far too few for a seat in the Dutch Parliament, but good enough to gain momentum for the change I, and many people with me, are aiming for.

I myself got life-jammed in 2008 (a term I use for people getting hopelessly stuck in live). At the moment of getting jammed, I had a life many people would probably desire for: For approximately seven years I had already been a successful interim manager at one of the nation's major commercial banks, had just bought a little farm with 1,5 acres of land, had a nice wife and daughter. My personal 'Major Depression' got me into the Dutch mental health care system, psychiatry, antidepressants (pills) and the so called 'anti-depression protocol'). It couldn't help me.

What was it that got me down? It was a combined set of factors which created my 'trap'. Some had to do with my own choices (eg. to buy this farm and take out a mortgage). Some had to do with bad luck: the housing market which started to collapse and the credit crunch emerging. And the fact my girlfriend found out she was pregnant just one week after signing the contract for the house (for 1,5 year we were trying to get pregnant).

I can state two things however with almost 100% certainty: One: I would not have tried to commit suicide without the mortgage. Two: The mental health care system as we know it was a primary reason for mysuicide attempt. This system enlarged my trap instead of easing it...

I attempted suicide in July 2008. I ended up in a psychiatric hospital. But... I left after five weeks and went to Biarritz (a small place at the Atlantic Ocean in France), and after that I went for a three weekhike in Corsica. I found my own cure. This was merely luck. Nothing more and nothing less. And it was the start of my own 'private investigations' (I used the title of the same named song of the Dire Straits). This song however describes my process in close accuracy: "Scared for life... I started my... Private... Investigations".

These investigations led primary to writing a book called 'Diagnosis Lifejam', describing the sickness of present mental health care system and pharma industry. But it also led to the insight that the reason of so many people getting 'depressed' has its roots in how our society has evolved itself. Out of about 17 million inhabitants of the Netherlandsthe Netherlands, approximately 1 million people take antidepressants each year. A clearer indicator of a sick harmonism, in this example our society, is almost impossible. These figures will not be much better in the rest of the world I am afraid...

Why is it, that our leaders, politicians, thinkers, writers, company directors do not take notice of this? Why is it that our society does not have the 'brains' to start an investigation itself to find out what the sick-making elements are? Why is it that the 'system' prefers to focus on the symptoms, insteadof healing the harmonism?

I want to change this world.

I came to the conclusion that I could write a book on the 'true essence' behind depression. That I could write a book on a far more healthy remedy for people who got into a 'major depression' than the 'path' the mental health care system offers.

I wrote that book. It is called 'Diagnosis Lifejam'.

But I felt that writing this book was only a (minor) part of the solution to help people and society. Rather than to cure individual people, I felt I should help to cure society as a whole. Cure the system.

Out of this necessity the Novaglobe book (and organisation) was born...

2.1 Systemjam, chaos point and world shift

Due to my work in the financial heart of ABN AMRO (one of the biggest banks in the Netherlands) I am very well introduced in the money system. My specialty was mortgages, risk management and capital regulations. I have seen that in the past 10 years at least three new regulations were defined and brought to practice in the financial system.

I also noticed that each new regulation measure only made things worse. Combined with the endless money creation by banks, greediness of managers and shareholders and more and more financial 'derivative' products, a self-destructive uncontrollable beast had been created.

This part of our ecosystem is malfunctioning. And we are not able to undo the damage done. To unfold it. The only thing which can help the ecosystem to survive is to create a new 'blood' system. A new currency system, which is kept completely separated from the 'old' system.

Because of my own personal crisis I took a deep insight into another fundamental ecological subsystem: mental health care. I came to the conclusion that this system is completely dysfunctional as well and will only evolve further in the wrong direction. It is not capable ofo restoring itself in a sound manner, due to the fact that it is already 'in too deep' and that its 'constructors' are sick. I refer people interested in this ecological subsystem to the 'Diagnosis Lifejam' book.

So this makes two main ecological subsystems system-jammed. Terminal.

Than I read the 'Chaos Point' by Ervin Laszlo. He states that in some years (this could be very well 2012) the 'chaos' in our ecosystem will be aggregated into such extend, that only a 'quantum leap' as Ervin calls it, can lead the system out of its 'jam'. His points of view fitted seamlessly in the way I saw it. This is why I, or better: 'we' (within Deniesa a growing group of change makers is gathering) decided to make the work and vision of Ervin Laszlo the basis of our change philosophy. We also believe -like Ervin- in a global consciousness and wisdom. Why reinvent the wheel? We are one...

So, for analysis on why a movement like Novaglobe is needed, we now can refer to the work of Ervin Laszlo. The Novaglobe movement does not focus on *why* we need to change, it focuses on *how* we can change. Within the Novaglobe group we redesign our society. A 'green field' design: imagine that we could design our society *without* considering the existing systems, rules, dogma's, religions, borders, etc. and how to get there in a controlled manner.

What would this world look like?

Only thinking in this free manner, we can design an ecosystem which fulfils the requirements of the quantum leap. And new words and concepts make the difference.

Why? Words are the carriers of our reality. Of our world. And words which form the key describers of ecological subsystems will always carry the load of years and years of usage in the old world. Or, these words may have gotten an incorrect bias or semantics. Therefore we need new words.

2.2 Iconomy shifting towards Flowconomy

A word which for example is not used as a construction term in Novaglobe is 'economy'. Nowadays, economy is about a focus on gaining material possession. And about scarcity (read the wikipedia definition on 'economy for example').

Whereas Novaglobe is about abundance for all... So, the basis under the word 'economy' -or better: its present twisted semantics- is completely in contrast with what we want to achieve in Deniesa. We cannot use that word as a 'carrier of change'.

I started to name our current product-creation and exchange system as 'Iconomy'. Where the 'i' derives from 'icon', I (me) or 'idiotes'. Idiotes is Greek for 'egoism'. I see the present economic model as a system focused on 'survival' of the fittest (physically or rationally), and a system based on fighting (competition). Why not work together as is already happening in for example the Wikipedia or development of open source based software systems as Linux and Ubuntu?

A term used for the alternative model within Deniesa is called 'Flowconomy'. The goal is to retain the good things about the economic model, but get rid of the negative sides. Read the chapter on Flowconomy for a more detailed elaboration on this topic.

And... the Flowconomy is <u>not</u> another *type* of economic model: It *replaces* economy.

The Flowconomy is <u>not</u> another *type* of economic model in the present sense: It *replaces* the present economical

implementation totally.

In the Zeitgeist Moving Forward movie, the current economical implementation has been qualified as in fact an *anti*-economy. When we take the semantics of the word 'economy' in its true sense, it is a good thing: it just means something as 'doing the household'. So the word and its implementation have been twisted and so make the word unusable as a design pillar. That is why the word 'Flowconomy' came into play.

And the *Iconomy* is typically denoted by keywords such are depicted in this Zeitgeist Movie screen shot:

Figure: Zeitgeist moving forward movie unveiling the truth about the economic implementation model (I label this model 'Iconomy' in this book, to make a clear distinction between the 'old' (no good) model, the anti economy, and a new possible model, called Flowconomy in this book). Time stamp in movie: 1 hour, 10 minutes. The Flowconomy model has no interest rates, no inflation, no loans, no money supply discussions.

And, for example in the Iconomy highly sustainable products (which is good?) are not 'economical', so, as a consequence of evolution of the system dynamics, we create products which do not last as long as they could, spoil the earth, are inefficient, etc. With the current economical model, this in unavoidable, even though many companies state they really have 'The Planet' high on the agenda, produce sustainable, etc'.

Figure: Zeitgeist Moving Forward, scene pointing out Product sustainability is inverse to economic growth...

As long as the Primary Iconomy Constructors (PIC)[2] are not taken out of the implementation, see the chapter by the same name later on, nothing will change and are all those words about producing more environmentally friendly, highly hypocrite and untrue. The Venus Project follows this line as well (more on the Venus Project in the redesign part in this book). The difference with the redesign posed in this book, is that we can already migrate towards it *now*, with presently available social and juridical structures. The people themselves can make it work, directly, simply by choosing other people and organisations to obtain their goods and services from, and leave employers which have PIC's as an underlying foundation of their company and head for PIC-less employers.

In the same movie, this speaker qualifies the economy a most bizarre delusion of our age. He is right... That is where the 'I' in Iconomy applies to as well: *Idiotery.*

[2] The Primary Iconomy Constructors are explained in more detail further on in this book, in the chapter 'Primary Iconomy Constructors'.

Figure: Zeitgeist moving forward, pointing out the delusion called 'economy'. Time stamp: 1 hour, 9 minutes.

2.3 About Heaven = Heav'n = Have Non

And speaking about abundance. Many books and articles talk about 'abundance'. That we should live in abundance. But where is it? I do not *see* abundance. Sorry.

Of course, when you are lucky you achieved a 'level' of spiritual abundance. 'In your head'. Could be. But when you open your eyes and experience the 'real world', for instance looking at the bills you have to pay, your children taking up most of your time,therefore leaving you hardly any time for 'yourself', the pressure you experience doing your job and earning your money, the negative news coverage of the newspapers... where is the abundance?

There will be no abundance if we do not reorganize our practical world...

So, why not *realise* it in our world? Realise John Lennon's

Imagine song? I -and many with me- experiencing more and more, that the way to practical abundance is *sharing*. At micro level: within a small group of people, within a city, but especially also at global level. Don't worry, you don't have to give up your 'belongings'. You may stay the 'guardian'. But you can share your things. And than things you desire for come to you. Don't worry, they will.

It might feel a little strange, that instead of accumulating things and keeping them for yourself to create abundance, the idea is the opposite. Share them or give things away. I have lived that way for the past 2,5 years now, and I can truely say: it works. The same goes for money: if you accumulate it to secure an abundant e retirement without money pressure, it will work the opposite. As we now are seeing with retirement funds breaking down and causing a lot of stress, especially to the elderly or people close to reaching retirement age.

A nice word-wisdom encryption came to me while wondering around at Lanzarote on a winters day. I was wondering what other words could be derived from the word 'heaven'.... Than I thought 'heaven' sounds like 'heavn' or have-non. Sounds like an unfinished clear sign for mankind: have-non is the way to heaven, or even better: they are similar. A sign of things to come. .

Something else remarkable is that another basic value is in there too: no pressure (pression). No obligation. No promises. More on that in the 'goodvalues' chapter.

As I mentioned before, I saw society as "sick". The Zeitgeist Moving Forward movie calls our social society sickness 'value system disorder'...

Figure: Zeitgeist moving forward, depicting our desire for 'things'. New things. Expensive things. The delusion that owning material goods makes us happy is fed by the Iconomy marketing machine. Time stamp in the movie: 1 hour, 3 minutes.

So, the way to abundance, and heaven on earth is... *have not*.

> "The way to abundance, and heaven on earth is... *have non*"

Another way of experiencing it: the word 'have' as in owning something., I see this as one as the most disagreeable words that exist. It has both 'you or i must' in it and 'possession'. In Dutch you need two words to express those -for me negative- things: "moeten" (must) and "hebben" (have). Strange, no?

And in the Netherlands there is a tendency to try to avoid the word 'moeten' (must). Mainly based on books of Eckhart Tolle ("Live in the moment") and growing desire and interest in the 'Buddhist way of Life'. Replacing 'must' by 'will' or 'would like to ' consequently sometimes gives some strange sentences, but it changes your life. It makes you really conscious of whether the things you do are your desire, are good for you, or are forced on you by your environment, and especially, 'the system'.

2.4 About the Squirrels and Ice Age...

A new flaw in the ecosystem has manifested itself in the Netherlands. The Netherlands are proud of their retirement system. For years, few other countries could state the buffers for retirement for the elderly to such an extend as the Dutch could.. but... it seems that these 'securities' are far less secure than economists and politicians stated until now. The first retirement funds which had to lower their pay outs have emerged.. And, knowing the dynamics of the financial system, the actual situation is probably far worse than this.

For the Dutch people this really was a first shock wave. Hopefully the notion that "the enemy is at the gate"' (as the Dark Riders were in the Shire, read Lord of the Rings by Tolkien) will wake people out of their sleep. I see parallels between Hobbits and Dutch people: they spend a lot of time taking care of their lawns, cutting the grass, clean their windows,but they do not take notice of the world melting down until it is... *almost* too late. And our leaders and politicians talk as Wormtongue and Saruman in 'Lord of the Rings'. They make us fall asleep (and themselves too I am afraid).

Our leaders tell us that *maybe* a second crisis is at hand.

I say we are *still* at the bottom of the *first* crisis and we are about to drop through the bottom. In the previous three years a deeper crisis has been avoided by lending billions and billions of Euros by our governments. The Dutch national debt has nearly doubled in a few years. The governments cannot do this again. They are out of ammunition. The next drop will be like an enemy breaking through defence lines with only unarmed women and mothers defending the village...

Thinking about what I am doing, and the previous example of the retirement funds, I suddenly recall the Ice Age movie. A little crack in the ice is the beginning of a total melt down of the habitat of the animals in the movie.

Only one animal sees the danger an tries to avoid it: a little 'stupid' squirrel. Other animals do not see the danger... the end of the story is that this little squirrel leads the whole group of animals into a new world.

I think we need a lot of 'stupid squirrels'. Only when you are "naive" enough to think we can really change our world you can gain energy and the vision to help realising it.

I am such a squirrel. I hope you are. Or will become one. I invite you to become one and join this venture... And since I 'woke up' and became a 'changemaker' I met numerous people who have been working on 'the good cause' for years. While working at the bank, I didn't notice the evil, which was at my hands too by supporting this system. I too was responsible for keeping it alive and letting it grow...

Figure: Deniesa's Mascotte, the Ice Age squirrel, coco nuts, holding a guitar, here at PowerFlower Studio's Garden, the Netherlands...

The good news however is that we only need a small group of squirrels to initiate the change needed...

These people do not want so sit in silence. Wait and see while 'the system' destroys the world (including nature) we are living in.

Deniesa is meant as one of those platform for people to meet, gain energy and inspiration and really start living the new world. Please take notice that Deniesa is 'just' one of the many initiatives already in existence. In similar ways we all started the probably biggest open source project ever. We can only do this together. And for everybody there is a role to play. If the people who truly desire it... Deniesa, especially is not meant to become a next institute or icon...

2.5 The speechless uniting...

"Where the speechless unite
In a silent accord
Using words you will find are strange
And mesmerised as they light the flame
Feel the new wind of change"
[Pink Floyd, On the turning away]

Change the system

"The change we desire is often said to be a change of mentality. A spiritual change after which all will change automatically. I believe this to be only partly true.

We can adapt a different mentality. Worldwide, this process is growing fast, mainly due to the Internet and (financial) crises, showing us the backside and 'truth' about our 'civilisation'. It also shows us that the price of economic growth is a price too high to pay, and is not making us any happier. And even worse: we can not even *maintain* our present level of welfare, the system is jammed and breaking down. The only way out of it is *fundamental change.*

A change of mentality is not enough. We need to change a lot of practical things as well. In the present *system* even good people create bad output. This is due to how the system works. So many people work for social departments, but more and more people they are supposed to help end up even worse, due to bureaucracy and a gradually changing twisted system. In other words: each one of the employees has good intentions and does 'his' job to the best of his abilities and 'follows' the rules, but the collective output *takes* value from our society instead of *adding* it. So good people and good intention bring misery due to a transformation of this intention via a twisted system. And nobody is to blame..

We *need* a new *system*. I do not believe in anarchy. We need an organisation. We need (want) guidelines. Note that I do not call them 'rules' or 'laws.

And we need emotion *and* logic to create it. That is why once the word 'spirilogic' was created. That is why the word 'reason' is important: it combines senses (emotion, the heart), values, and logic (the head, the thinking).

The banking sector is not going to bring the required 'quantum leap', because it would need to terminate itself before it could.. The same is true for psychiatry,politics, our economic system, the government, etc, etc. The system does not innovate any more and it is stretched to its maximum proportions. System jam.

> The current discussion in the USA about the so-called 'debt limit' is a symptom of a corrupt system stretched to its maximum proportions.

The system needs to change to such an extend that people working in this system will experience it as if their careers, safety and futures have been destroyed by it. They will feel there lives are ruined However, looking at it from a holistic point of view, this is untrue. They might not be aware of it yet, but they will be freed from the system too. The crux is to create a new safe place for them before the system breaks down completely...

The only way out of this situation is a huge crash (melt down), or the creation of a new system. I choose the latter. The crash variant will be a process without any control or sensible guidance, probably ending up in a lot of misery, going far beyond the Great Depression of the 1930's. The creation of a new system will be a tough path too, but can be done in a controlled way. Step by step. Building the new system and implementing it on the one hand, and avoiding a total crash on the other. That is the idea.

"The only way out of this situation is a huge crash (melt down), and/or the creation of a new system."

The change will be initiated by forces which are minimally *connected* or *dependent* on the system. People who work or act *in* the system are stuck, cannot move (yet). Their employer and environment will punish them directly for stepping out of line.

I met so many people (hired consultants AND employees), while working in the banking industry, who say different things in private to what they say in public. They have fear for losing their jobs. And they are right. I hope more and more people will stand up, and join the change. Find a way to step out of the system, or at least contribute less to it, which is difficult, I know...and dare to speak their mind and what they believe in, in public. Let this be their call...

At the March 21 2011 Club of Budapest meeting, I rose the question how to make all those potential change leaders free of the existing system. They too are bound by needing to raise money for their family, mortgage, etc... As long as we do not provide for this, an enormous potential is left untouched.

Where are the change makers?

I think therefore that the change will be led primary by entrepreneurs (not tied by an employer - employee contract), artists, the 'weak and poor', the 'young' and hopefully the elderly will join too.

I foresee that people who now 'possess' much will be the ones having the hardest time the coming years. Especially the ones with a mortgage, debts, or owning big company structures (with a lot of employees). The reason for this is that without this 'weight' one can easily change towards a new world. Structures will start breaking, because the debt-based economy cannot continue any longer. And it will take many people, years and years to accept that they cannot stop the water, and better start swimming or jump on the boat (and leave the many things they got attached to at the bottom of the sea).

People who 'own' a lot, or even worse, have a debt, probably need many years to first get rid of this 'burden'... All lost energy. People who are not in this situation can directly start building and moving in a new system. That is why I think Africa is the continent holding the best playing cards for the time to come. This continent has withstand the Western Debt and Capitalism Virus far better than other continents.

Time will tell.

About entrepreneurs

And with entrepreneurs in this context, I mean people who subcontract themselves to companies and government for their services. In the Netherlands the Netherlands more and more of those sole proprietorships (their juridical format is that of a company) arise.

Entrepreneurs can step out of the system which we want to change more freely than employees or employers. And entrepreneurs are mostly gifted with a talent for 'organising' things and put them to action. The only problem is that they - at this moment- too, depend on the system for *money,* they too have a family to raise, food to buy and make sure they have a roof over their heads. So, an important step in the migration is to make people less dependent on money from the system.

> An important step in the migration is to make people less dependent on money from the system.

About artists

Artists have retained maximum creativity and an open look on the world. The majority has always stayed 'poor' and thus did not get trapped in the system with a mortgage, expensive car and a lot of window dressing. They are used to live without possession. They can imagine a world in which much possession only has a minor role. They just want to do their thing, and on average they do care far less about money (as a thing to accumulate) than most people. People who have never been an artist themselves, can seldom understand that way of life...

They do not have to be afraid of loosing all their material belongings, because they hardly have any. did not many banks granted them loans or mortgages, so they are far less likely to be bound by debt than the average person.

About the 'weak' and the 'poor'

And what to think about all those people who are now classed as the 'weak' and the 'poor'? People spending there time in mental institutions because they cannot or will not be part of this society? What about the homeless? What about all those people who dropped out of the system without a job, but are tied by the 'social care' departments, so they cannot do anything useful (in the Netherlands you loose your social welfare rights quite easily if you try to do something useful in society, because the system than assumes you can 'work'). All those people on social benefit because they are not 'suitable' for work. Can't they they do something useful for society?

Don't they *want* to be useful to? Often they do, but they too are trapped in the system: not able to work in the system (Iconomy game), and thus considered unable to do anything at all... I work a lot with this kind of people (young and old), and I have experienced that if you let them do things in their own pace, and create an environment of trust and non-competition, they can create and produce the most beautiful things. So, are they sick, or is our working arena maybe sick? I think the latter.

Young people

There is one category of free people I did not mention yet: young people. These people often still have a free spirit. They are no yet locked in all days pression of the combination of raising children, working, being in debt (mortgage) and having house prices fears.

In the Netherlands the government created a system in which students can go to college but they will be left with a huge debt. The system is designed to place everyone in debt. This is not the way. Fewer people should fall into debt, not more. Read the Flowconomy chapter for more of this.

Young people see their future ruined by the previous generation(s). They start their lives with a huge national debt. They cannot buy or rent a house any more. They pay the bill. Are they willing to do so? Is it fair they pay the bill?

I don't think so. And the only way to avoid it is to move to a new system. In which the national debt is left a debt. Bury it. Do something reasonable with all the material goods we created in this world. They remain, even if we make the debt disappear, surely.

The old order is rapidly fading...

"And admit that the waters
Around you have grown
And accept it that soon
You'll be drenched to the bone.
If your time to you
Is worth savin'
Then you better start swimmin'
Or you'll sink like a stone
For the times they are a-changin

...

For the loser now
Will be later to win
For the times they are a-changin

...

The order is
Rapidly fadin'.
And the first one now
Will later be last"

[Bob Dylan, The Times they are A Changing]

The people mentioned in previous paragraphs are typically the same people who in previous times did not feel like stepping into politics. Or to raise their voice. They where the 'speechless'. But they feel they are called now. They feel that they have to move. I see more and more people stepping up. And taking on a role nobody had expected they could or want to fullfil. These people are often very aware of what is happening in society. They know, and certainly feel it. And the internet, the social media give them the possibility to speak, communicate with others, to unite, to gain energy and step up.

We live in wonderful times...

The change will be led by the 'ordinary'.

About the BOMb and World War III
In this section I want to tell you about a - for me - useful view point with regards to our companies and government based system, and why I feel the third world war has already started...

BOMb stands for **B**usiness g**O**vernment hu**M**an

About business

As stated earlier: for about 10 years I have been working in the banking industry as a consultant. I have been walking around wearing a suite and tie. I have seen and taken part in vendors telling lies to customers to sell there products. And everybody has to, or theywill not survive in this business to business competitive environment.

Lies and deceit has become normal business ethics. I have seen and experienced the devastation hedge funds and stock market driven dynamics bringing companies down. Companies being torn in two. Everybody fighting for themselves to survive. People become beasts... wearing suits. No, it is even worse: beasts do not know what they are doing, and kill only to eat, if need be. People kill for money, material and destructive ego... I experience my personal crash in 2008 as a direct consequence of these 'commercial dynamics'. Why did this have to happen? So many people experience the same, and the numbers will only rise in the coming period.

I now know what is is like to be in depth due to the dynamics of money, the monetary system. I burned myself on it...

And I noticed how companies get rid of employees that are no use to them anymore. They swallow them, chew them upand spit them out. Only after this has happened a person notices that it is too late. And there is no alternative...

About the government

After this period I was involved in a project for the Department of Economics, it focused on streamlining and optimising the Rotterdam harbour (one of the biggest transport / exchange harbours in Europe). The Dutch government board decided they wanted to reduce the government's 'overhead' for companies with about 10%. One of the places was the harbour: it took containers sometimes weeks to pass through customs , due to tax procedures, etc. People thought they could optimise the process, by putting an information system around it.

To my opinion they did not do something about the real cause, which I call the 'business-government complex'. The parties involved in the logistics do not *want* to cooperate with each other. For instance: there was a 'checkpoint' company which did all kinds of examination on the containers. This 'function', the government had 'privatised' (sold) some years earlier. Long queues of trucks had to wait for hours each day to get their inspection. This company -I just focussed on making profit- had no intention to cooperate in optimising the whole logistic chain. Why should it? The queues made sure that their business went like a train: they always looked busy, no 'idle time', etc.

And the 'government' institutions (tax department, customs and the authority responsible for quality), did they give 'a damn'? It didn't feel that way. I experienced breathtaking bureaucracy, fear for saying things, stupidity, etc. A result of the 'Misery Creating Syndromes (see the appendix with this name). Their salaries are taken care of by the tax payer.

And, of course, people here are 'victims' of the system too. Working in such an environment for about 10 years will make you apathetic, or sick, or you will leave... so, what kind of people are left there after say 30 years system evolution, let say 100 years?

And the project I worked for? It was carried out by a group of about 40 interim consultants each one of them earned approximately 100 to 120 Euros an hour. About 100.000 Euros to 200.000 Euros per annum , which is about the salary of the Dutch prime minister They didn't mind at all that the programme would take years and years. They really thought -or so it felt- they did a great job. I only saw millions of Euros waisted and saw a non-functioning process getting stuck in the mud even further by sealing it into an ICT system... Idiotic. And when I proposed to take care of the real underlying problems, it was made pretty clear I should mind my own business. Asking critical question about this subject could affect highly placed people, stakes, relations and internal government politics. So, let us continue to make this stupid system even more stupid and bigger and waste even more tax money.

That made me wonder... what is it, that makes this system jam, what is it? Why is it, that despite all these talents,good intentions and so much money, it only gets worse?

It seemed that the 'commercial' parties working for profit (I call them 'Business' in this book), and the people who work and pay taxes, where entangled in some destructive dance. A destructive dance, based on ego wanting power and prestige, people and companies demanding more profit, people not willing to give up there place for the sake of the group, etc.

In Dutch the expression 'DHOEM' raised in my mind. Standing for (in Dutch) 'Destructieve Homeostase OverhEid-Marktwerking'. In other words and in English: our capitalistic system in which we separate production systems in two categories: Government and Business, is so much entangled that it is not able to generate prosperity and growth any more. In the Netherlands, even one of the country's largest banks (ABN AMRO) is owned by the government. So what type of organisation is this organisation? Government or Business? And how can it compete with 'pure' business banks (who's stocks are not owned by the state), in a fair way? That is impossible, due to the fact that ABN AMRO is backed up by the state. So it will always get a more positive credit rating by agencies as Moody's, and thus can get money at the capital market at far lower costs...

'Homeostase' stands for 'equilibrium', or 'stable state'. And what I mean in this case, is that it is an ongoing destructive state.

Business and Government entered in a hybrid complex, which is not able to generate more prosperity for the people. It even declines.

OK, a lot of complex words and concepts. What I want you to remember is that a division in 1. Government and 2. Business, makes sense, to understand, and even more important, *redesign* our world.

Watching the Zeitgeist movie(s), I noticed that this division is used too. Government and business (or companies). This , to my mind is probably useful to understand system dynamics.

Of course there are other important groups like the religious movements, these I will not address at this moment. They are irrelevant to the systemjam I am talking about right now.

Government and business areas are there to serve us humans. Not the other way around (as I feel is happening right now, we are marionettes of the 'system'). So, the third player comes in: the human.

I found this model of three elements very useful in understanding what's happening in our economy. But it proved also a very good model to understand why politics does not function (anymore).

As a resume, we have:

1. The Business (B)
2. The gOvernment (O)
3. The huMan (M)

Note: the reason I take the B, the O and the M, is to keep it synchronous with the Dutch terms: Bedrijfsleven (Business), Overheid (Government) and Mens (Human). Forming the word 'BOM' in Dutch, meaning bomb in English. And I find this acronym very appropriate: 'Mother, when will they drop the bomb?" [Pink Floyd]. Or, when does the Bomb explode? When does the system jam reach its outer limits and halts completely? Or in a more positive way: when do we 'drop' this model (drop the bomb).

Is it useful to make a division between 'government' and 'business' in the new world at all?

I see 'government' and 'business' taking over each other functions by 'evolution', or even better: they seem to merge. Maybe this is a natural and good direction anyway, and is it high time to remove the 'boundaries' which block a total merge, and make that the 'de facto' merge, which is highly inefficient, fades.

This subject will be dealt with in this book, in the parts concerning the redesign.

As I see it, the government (O) and Business (B) should serve the human (M). The BO-System is jammed to such an extent, that it has a severe effect on people, and sucks the energy out of them (more and more taxes, more and more rules and laws, more and more pressing loans, more and more a consumers economy destroying nature, etc).

And yes, the strange thing is that the BO-System is driven by... the very same group: people. People are driving a killing car. Good people walk into this killing machine and unintentionally begin to give negative value to the world. When good people walk into this machine, they become the parts, the driving force, and end up as brothers fighting brothers. In competing companies, but also via all kinds of 'social organisations' which should help the weak and the poor, but often only make things worse.

And nobody wants this to happen, but still it does. And it grows, the evil,bad side in society grows day by day. Like a cancer, killing the human body supporting it.

I see this as the third world war. And 1984 (George Orwell). . But this time, the war is not fought at distant battlefields. The war takes place right under our nose. It is the employer firing his employee because of the crisis. It is the seed of anger, jealousy and fear between employees, who is next to be fired or promoted. It is the lying politician. It is the raping religious extremist. It is the young family not having enough time and dedication for their children because of daily stress in order to reach the end of the month. Parents battling with their children in fact. It is also the couples who want to split up and divorce, but cannot do this because of a mortgage...

I can name hundreds of examples, of mini-bombs exploding within our midst. When we start to see it? But the enemy, who is the enemy? That is difficult part, we cannot see it, because we are our own enemy. It is our destructive emotion, combined with the destructive elements in our ecosystem causing it.

When will they see, when will the learn?
[Madonna, Live to tell]

That is how the system dynamics work nowadays. That is how a destructive economy-implementation works. In this book, I call this destructive economy with all of its elements 'Iconomy'. And it is important to know, to see, that the government as we know it, is an element of that system. We cannot understand or cure the system, without underpinning the role of the government.

Iconomy is the present destructive form of our economy. It mainly consists of a 'business' area (especially companies with stock market notation) *and* our government, including 'politics'.

Economy is not wrong in itself (it means 'housekeeping', the same goes for 'system'. The present *implementation* of these concepts have become wrong. To denote that *implementation* I use the word '*iconomy'.*

In an Iconomy the 'I' takes over the 'we'. It is about egoism and idiots (these terms are synonym in Greek). In other words: stupidity.

And I haven't even mentioned the government which makes employers and employees fight each other with lawyers, via 'work / social security departments' (this happens in the Netherlands). Lawyers like this. Lawyers like rules and idiocy. Their job is entwined with it...

And I haven't even mentioned a mental health care which puts a 'wall' between somebody breaking down and its environment. I only recently came to notice that psychiatric hospitals resemble macro isolation-cell like things. Nice to separate people from each other. And with this the psychiatric-pharmaceutical system profits[3]. And thus destroying the natural healing power of a cohesive and sound society.

I haven't mentioned the 'fear and sell' methods of companies to sell their products (Producers Syndrome).

Good, enough on these symptoms. As stated earlier, I want this book primary to be about a solution, and not about problems. If you are interested in how system dynamics work, watch the Zeitgeist movie (www.zeitgeistmovie.org, free download).

The 'core' of 'stupid' things happens in the kernel of the 'power': at the governments departments, at the head offices of multinationals. So, only few people actually see it. But more and more people become aware of it. The Iconomy cannot hide it any more. Because 'problems' (eruptions) are to big to camouflage, and because of the Internet (wikileaks for example). Transparency is the biggest enemy of Idiots. Stupidity and badness (dark things), cannot remain in the light. They will fade.

The problem is however, that the 'stupid' things which the 'chiefs' do at the top have a big consequence for the 'ordinary': they lose a job, end up in debt, loose security or even their food. So, high time the 'ordinary' start to move and raise their voices...

One good thing: we can heal our world. This book describes a different world. With a system. But with a constructive system. If enough people want it to happen, it will happen. Or

[3] If you wish, you are invited to read more about de psychiatric malfunction in the book 'diagnosis lifejam' (Dutch: Diagnose Levensklem, www.levensklem.nl).

maybe it has already happened... maybe we already passed the tipping point and heading in the good direction?

2.6 How to get there: quantum leap– Ervin Laszlo

The new society cannot be constructed by only doing 'a part' of it. All subsystems (law, politics, monetary system, etc.) are to much entangled for that. Trying to only change a part will leave you in a disillusioned state soon. And it cannot be done country by country. Everything is connected. One big conglomerate.

Each time a (sub) system changes, it sinks deeper into the swamp. Like a fish working itself deeper and deeper in the fishing trap.

Making a wrong system better is still doing steps into the wrong direction...

Fundamental change can only be realised by organised step by step migration process. Detach a part and connecting it to the new system. And making sure that the old system (Iconomy) does not lay its tentacles upon the newborn seeds and squash them. And, at the same time, the store should remain open, while rebuilding it. We cannot shut down the economy totally while rebuilding it.

I did a lot of these total redesign and migration projects at banks. Who could have known this experience will be very useful in the time to come...? I am happy that working all these years at these -I feel now- 'bad institutes' had a reason and serves society.

About the term 'quantum leap'. I wasn't the one who introduced it. I got this term from Ervin Laszlo. In his book 'Chaos Point' he makes very clear why the change will go via a quantum change. And not via a moderate pace. I agree totally with him. In the next paragraph I will address the reason for a quantum leap-like change in short.

Read this book. And watch Zeitgeist Moving Forward (free down loadable at www.zeitgeistmovie.org) and you know enough...

2.7 'The System': 200 years of 'legacy code', spaghetti

I am graduated as information engineer at a University in the Netherlands. And I have done or participated in about 100 projects within banking industry. All had a business-process, people, and software (computer programmes) component in them. And probably about 90% had a migration focus: going from one organisation with corresponding processes to to another.

Each time the question rose "Are we gonna change the software of the facilitating ICT-system, or do we throw it away and rebuild it?". A rule of thumb in the information industry is that once a software system has reached a substantial size (lines of code), a high complexity, and the software has a high degree of 'spaghetti code', it would be very wise to rebuild the whole system from scratch. Certainly not trying to rebuild it. Many, many projects have ended up trying to change parts of computer programmes over and over again. One step forward, to steps back. Each piece of rope you take away unleashes a whole number of unexpected defects in other parts of the system. Hopeless.

The same goes for our society 'system'. But than the lines of code are the the rules, regulations, laws, procedures, all kinds of functions, a far too complex financial system, etc. No longer possible to change in a profound way.

Remember that our 'system' is at least 200 years old. And we never decided to clean up and restart. Now we have all kinds of strange rules, even zombie rules (without a clear requirement of owner). We have subsystems which were constructed around ideas and technology of two centuries ago (our political system). And we cannot change it in a profound reasonable way. In ICT terms: we have a lot of legacy. And having a lot of legacy is not good: it can even be terminal for an organisation. It becomes a burden. The organisation cannot change in a sound way, following the new circumstances. And that is what is happening...

When it is really big spaghetti, you cannot even do minor adjustments, not even if you would hire a thousand programmers. Managers often say: well, just hire more programmers. Put in more money. Often, managers aren't as smart, as they want us to believe... All those programmers will make things worse; they stop to cooperate, sit in each others way, etc.

I think the infrastructure system serving our society (government + economy) got stuck so badly, that this is the case. We can't even change minor things any more. The only way is down. Why the only way is down, I will address in chapter "Primary Iconomy Constructors". It has to do with underlying structuring factors...

Once again the comparison with a computer system: often documentation is gone. And nobody knows what certain programmes do or are connected with. Nobody dares to change the system, afraid it will break down. The same goes for our society system: government staff don't dare to change or erase a rule, afraid that in some other part of the government it will make break down things. Or that somebody will make them accountable for a 'failure'.

2.8 From 'Imagine' to 'Realising'

This book has been written with inspiration from many books. The ideas of many are in it. I do not believe that all these ideas are mine. . I believe in a collective consciousness, in practical terms connected via the internet. So this book is also a part of your creation. I see myself only as a medium. The lucky one writing it down. In the same context, I do not believe in copyright as we know it. I believe for instance that 'pop stars' are the lucky ones who got the inspiration (inspiration means 'being in the breath gods').

It is not good that they take advantage of it by aggregating so much money and goods out of this. This is not living modestly. They should feel gifted. Actually, they are the ones who should give away... not take. At last that is my opinion. Of course the community should make sure they can do their thing in a nice way. But that is it. That is modesty. That is nobility.

Let's carry on with this book. I realise that many will say I am a lunatic, a dreamer. The only thing I hope is that you will join me. And one day, I hope that many will say I was a realist, back then. And only a few remain dreaming... Think of the Imagine song of John Lennon. Imagine. Realise we can do it. Realise we can create the world John Lennon is singing about. Replace each time 'imagine' by 'realising', and it becomes true.

I encounter quite a few people who say things will find their way without their efforts to change it. That 'politicians' will take care of it. And that we have economists and other wise people who are specialists in these topics. If it was that bad, they would mention it and take care of it, don't you think?

No.

In this book you will find out why they *won't* take care of it. They cannot take care of it. That is logic. These people (or maybe better: their roles) make up the Iconomy. Or these people heavily depend on the Iconomy to retain their wealth, power or destructive ego.

I hope all people will start to place the newspaper headings in a different light. As I mentioned before, I have been working in the banking sector for approximately ten years, . I know what the Zeitgeist movie is about. I am a witness. I know that many, who haven't been eye witness of how the 'economy' works, will have difficulties to understand the system. The Iconomy.

But once you see the mechanics, the dynamics of how stock markets, profit making, ego's, destructive emotions, politicians and power interact, you will start to see patterns in the newspaper headings. You start to correlate your own life and the Iconomy system. You will feel it too. I hope. You will see the 'constructors' of the Iconomy.

Why not?

We all are the architects of our future. The future is ours. We can change this world. Imagine you had a white canvas, and *you* where the designer of a new world, what would it look like? And don't listen to the people saying 'yes, but...'. There is no 'but'. The canvas is blanc. Try it.

I think there are many among us, who see the writing on the wall already. And quite some who've seen it for much longer than I have. But they are waiting for the proper words. They are waiting for a change organisation to synergize their powers and vision with. That is where Novaglobe intends to lend a helping hand (especially all local subsidiaries). These people wait for a simple and compact design of the new world. Which is coherent and holistic. That is what this book aims for. It is not aimed to be perfect or 'ready'. Like a design, it can and will alternate during time. But without a design, without a plan we cannot work together, and realise the new world... So, this is a call for all those system designers and architects out there to join.

We need a spot on the horizon to aim for. To set our course.

And, maybe even more important: we need a transition path. A road map. I have been to three Zeitgeist III performances at cinemas. So many people, after watching the movie, were saying: "OK, I understand the system, we should change, but how? What can I do?". Together with the Zeitgeist / Venus project movement we intend to make a realistic road map. A stairway to heaven. To have non. To a world without the money as we know it. Without the Iconomy.

The past two years many, many people said to me: "Iwanjka, what you say is not possible". And each time I asked: "Why not?". And some times I adjusted the plan, the vision in my mind. But more and more often, the discussion ended in silence. And I felt a resonance hanging around: "It can be done...". The good thing is that this design has been 'tested' by a lot of intelligent and critical people. The first test round is ready.

And the same things people said to me when I started to write a book on the mental care system and psychiatry: "You? Writing a book is difficult you know, you have to study for that...". And than: "You want to join national elections, you? You can't do that", and six months later we joined the elections, did a thing with a lot of people, which was thought impossible.

So, if all this can be done, why not realise that new world? I know, I feel, you and I can realise it.

Together.

2.9 New words and new books make the difference

The way to the new world is a road we are going to construct ourselves. Nobody is gonna tell you how (Madonna, 4 minutes to save the world song). We cannot use the present models in politics or society. These ideas and models have served their time. They showed and show that they do not work any more.

It is time to re-evolute. To create a new plateau.

As long as we keep talking about a concept labelled 'economy', like "We should create another economic model", we make our own restrictions . And that is not because the word 'economy' is wrong in its original sense, meaning 'doing a household'. But nowadays it is directly connected with concepts such as 'BBP growth', 'interest rates', 'inflation', etc. In other words: it is tight to the concept of money as we know it, the Business world as we know it, and the Government as we know it. Take a look on the 'economy' definition in the wikipedia example. When I did that, the element 'scarcity' in its definition made me see the light: I want to live in a world of abundance, so the present definition of word 'economy' does not fit in there anymore.

I have been breaking my head over a new term. A term that really expressed what I felt about a new production and exchange system in the new world. Words like 'weconomy' and 'givonomy' came close. But the feeling of creation of 'flow' in all dimensions made me choose for the word 'Flowconomy'. Which makes in its sound very clear that for instance a government should minimally mingle in the flow and creation of things. And this is what governments do a lot. The question is why they do it a lot. Then you come to the essence of what I call Iconomy. Other things have to change as well to avoid the 'Business sector' getting out of hand... more about that further on in this book Nearly every time I suggest ideas on another political or economical system people directly say I must be a communist. I invite people to use their creativity and create, design a new system themselves. Thinking out of the box. Not a communist or a capitalist system. We are creative and intelligent species, aren't we? Why not create a new system? But without naming that new system it remains vague and always ends up in the row of already existing names and systems. So, use new names!

Giving a definition of a subsystem a new name, a new label, makes it possible that with one word, other people know what you mean. And we do not have to use books to define what we mean, and so make it harder to go forward and create a system based on those new concepts. And even more important, it withholds us from starting to realise it.

Put in a more quantum mechanical - spiritual way: everything is energy and vibrations. So a spoken word is a capsule of manifestation. Speaking new words, which don't have the burden of a past, and a connection with old world, makes it possible to manifest a new reality...

In addition we need creative and innovative book writers, who write outside the box and dare to speak what they see and feel. These books can form the basis of the new world. Books about analysis of the old world: what works and what does not work,books on the design or building plans of the new world or both subjects in the same book. Both are crucial and necessary, so come on, in this age everybody can be a book writer. I never expected that I would write books. It is written in the stars that those from whom we expect it the least , will be the leaders of change....

Feel free to contact me if you have an idea of writing a new book, have a manuscript or a book ready. At the Novaglobe website we intend to publish a list of books, associated with one or more eco-subdomains (see design part), which we find change leading and innovative. Your book can be on that list... really, jut contact us...

2.10 How to read this book

This book mainly consists of three parts:

1. Analysis
2. Design

3. Implementation

You can read each part separately, but there are cross references.

I you are already familiar with how 'the system' functions, you can skip the 'analysis' part and continue directly with the Design and Implementation parts.

3 Deniesa wakes...

Deniesa is sitting in the attic of the house and watches the world through a little window. "I really don't understand what's happening, she mumbles...". Our political leaders are talking about living true values, and virtues. But why do they lie? Well, at least she has the feeling that they are lying, or at least they don't make things transparent which surely are relevant for her life. They seem to lie about banks, about the economy and, hummmm, what don't they lie about?

And why is it that we have to work longer hours. And more 'efficient', maybe even until we are seventy years old, whilst we are pretty sure that ongoing technological improvement should make us work less? How can it be? There must be something wrong somehow, somewhere, but what is it? Where is it?

Thankfully our leaders say: "We should take care, we do not enter a crisis like this one ever again...". Deniesa thinks: "I didn't notice the previous crisis was over...?".

Wondering song [Artist - Jaap]:

"Wondering about this world
Which is suffering in so many ways
Despite the good intentions
Of people everyday

Money, spent for elections
Money, spent everyday
Only the right direction
Is forced a different way

Why is this all happening
To us, I can't explain
I pray, is this the answer?

Why, we still relay?

Wondering, about this girl...
She is suffering... every day
Misguided... by destruction
People call her insane...

Why, is this all happening
To her, I cannot explain
I pray, it will be answered
In the silence, perhaps,
It may, it may, it may...
Wondering"

Than, suddenly, she sees the light... aha! Eureka! "I get it...". On the one hand she is happy she finally sees why things go as they go. On the other hand, it does not make her happy. A friend asks hers if she has seenthe Zeitgeist movie. She had not seen it yet, and decides to go and watch it. The movie fits perfectly in her vision of a different, new 'system'. The Venus project, which the movie poses as a solution, feels good in a certain way, but she finds it so sterile, and she does not see how to get there.

After the first feelings of euphoria, another feeling is filling her thoughts... things are really, really bad. Where can she go? It seems that 'the system' is melting down, and there is no place to escape from this global meltdown.

Visions of the news of America go through her head: people sleeping in ghettos next to the river. They are the victims of a 'foreclosure': they couldn't pay the interest of their debts, called mortgages. And the banks made them leave their houses, or they decided to leave themselves. "How evil, how silly..." she thinks, "and those houses remain empty?". And she thinks about a story, of Iwanjka a friend of hers. About a small country called 'the Netherlands'. In America people often send the key of their house to the bank, and then they are relieved of the debt of the house. In the Netherlands this is not possible. The debt will follow the people, even into their tents. And things are even worse: those Dutch people created a system that about the half of the interest you pay, is paid by the State, as long as you have a job. "Crazy! She thinks, what happens when those people loose their jobs? Their income gets divided into two and the interest they pay doubles??? Huhhh?". She starts to feel queasy. This could become very, very painful for those people. Iwanjka called it 'DutchDouleur'. The burden these people will have to carry because of closing their eyes, and let them be blinded by words of politicians and economists, and there own desire to posses a thing called 'a house'.

"But why is it that the political leaders and economists do not say something about this?", she asked Iwanjka. Iwanjka answered that admitting that this system is not sustainable is something similar to "We economists were wrong, the whole time". Big egos and tunnel vision, and the manifestation cramp of institutes will make the train only run faster and faster into the ravine. And the banking system, it is practically totally based on loans for houses. The banks will collapse swiftly once people will notice that their house -once 'bought' under a "come for your freedom" screaming advertisements- will prove to be a prison. A huge, huge burden. The opposite of freedom. And causing an enormous amount of stress. Zeitgeist is present, that's for sure.

And looking to the far West, she sees America. She has read about cities in America that had sent home all government staff; firemen, police, etc. But still, the citizens of the city had to pay city taxes... people asked for the reason and were answered that it was needed to pay for interest on the debt of the city... So slowly, but at a faster and faster pace, all the tax we are paying ends up in the mouth of banks...

"That's strange!", Brigitte, an artist and friend of her said, when she told her about these cities. Brigitte mostly has a clear vision on system things, but seldom understands them. Brigitte often tells of entrepreneurs who got a lot of money from the bank. Those people were able to buy all kinds of goods, to set up their business. She wasn't able to do that because she firmly dislikes borrowing money. She finds it strange that this 'good behaviour' is punished by the system. She does not want to take out a loan. As a consequence she has to work many, many hard hours for very little money. This really frustrates her, but she is not able to change it...

"That is strange", Deniesa thinks,"Good behaviour is not rewarded in this country!". "Brigitte is right".. Thatis one thing she is sure of She combines Brigitte's situation with the cities in America paying the entire city taxes directly to banks as interest, a cold feeling rises that there is something deeply wrong with the system of lending and borrowing money..

Another friend of hers, Raoul, who has been working for years in the fields of accountancy once tried to explain to her how it all works. Loans, money and banks.

It was all about money creation. "But how does this work then?", she often asked him. "What is the reason that banks make new money, when there seems to be enough of it already?".

Raoul explained to her that banks need to create new money in order to let people be able to pay the interest for the loans they have taken out. And that this is a vicious circle. Banks will go bankrupt once they stop creating new money. But... the tricky part is that money creation goes at a faster and faster pace. A money machine which is spiralling out of control, and has started to overheat.

Another thing Raoul explained was that banks are allowed to lend people about ten times the amount of money which they have themselves. Deniesa starts thinking: "So, imagine I have

1000 euro, then I am allowed to let people take a loan of 10.000 euro?". "And, I can ask for instance 10% of interest each year? And, then I get my total possession as interest *each year*?". "Yup", Raoul says. "And even worse: as soon you lend 10.000 euro, you have created 10.000 euro". "Ahhhh, so that's how it works... the money creation thing. ", Deniesa things... finally I get it. "And", Raoul says "that interest of 1.000 euro has to be created by banks too, because it did not exist before the client had to pay the interest". "That is strange", Deniesa thinks...

"And maybe the most creepy part of it", Raoul says, "is the way the money creation slips into our lifes. It is through inflation. Economist state that inflation is intrinsic to the economic system. That is not true, it creates new money". "So, if we did not create money, we would not have inflation?". "Probably not, or at least less", Raoul says. "So, inflation is not an integral part of economy?", Deniesa asks. "This depends whether lending money is part of the definition of 'economy'. Currently it is."

"But then, why do we create money?", Deniesa asks. Raoul: "Because a long time ago banks discovered that they could get more money out of there possession. And governments where asleep, or where part of the conspiracy".

Deniesa is confused. One moment she thinks she gets the point, another moment she is completely baffled. Feels like black magic, that money system. It is bizarre that banks make money, and that as a consequence the money in the hands of people reduces in value. Feels a bit like steeling. Could it be that those robust positioned institutes steel from the people. Deniesa really feels sick of the whole thing. But she thinks that this system will fail sooner or later... and that at some stage we will only pay interest to banks, or in a more camouflaged way the money in our pockets will get less and less due to the money creation of banks. On way or another more and more of the value we create goes directly in the pockets of banks.

Ding dong...

The American cities giving all their tax income away in the form of interest to banks... these are the examples of the jam the whole world is heading for.Raoul: "That is exactly what I am talking about...".

And then there is Iwanjka, the other friend. He has been working at banks for about 10 years. In 2008 he found himself totally jammed. He said he had a lot of stress because of a mortgage, of the fear of the housing market going down and leaving his family with a huge debt. He knew, because it was his working area, that banks had the right to force you to pay big sums of money directly when your house went down in value. People seldom realise the consequences of these 'small letters' in the signed contract.

Nobody believed him. Psychiatry labelled him depressive, burnout and gave him some other psychiatric labels. 'Diagnoses' they called them. He nevr wanted to call himself 'depressed', because he felt this was not the case, and that the 'cure' the mental care system offered was complete nonsense, at least in his case.

It ended up in a suicide attempt, mid 2008. He ended up in a psychiatric hospital. He was 'lucky', they could sell their house just before the housing market in the Netherlands started to crumble. He wrote a book on what happened to him, called 'Diagnosis Lifejam". In fact, his situation was fairly simple to grasp.However, the mental health system does not like simple solutions, because that would mean they would not be able to sell pills anymore and label people with difficult diagnoses.

Now Iwanjka often sings a song called 'Systemjam'. He rents an apartment. He says he intends never, never to take out a loan anymore. "Debt almost killed me"... if I ever, ever buy a house again, it will be without a mortgage...

The story of Raoul about a system jam coming... feels like Iwanjka's lifejam. But than a life jam for all people on earth, who are depending on our economic system. She decides to ask Iwanjka about his vision on it all.

Iwanjka agrees totally with her. "Yes, that what happened to me, is going to happen to a lot of people. Unfortunately". "And to the whole the country, and yes probably the whole world". "And the government-psychiatrists, the economists, only know about one antidepressant: create more money. Take on more debt."

"And like what happened to me, pills are not the answer. Only a real transition can do the trick. A reorganisation of our ecology is going to help. Like a company needs restructuring when it loses money year after year. In the same way I believe that in 90% of the major depression cases a reorganisation of a person's life is the only answer,not pills.".

Deniesa wonders... "And the problem is, like psychiatrists who cannot see through the mist of illusion that they where wrong for so many years, in the same manner economists and politicians cannot see through this mist of illusion. They are wrong. They have been pushing the country in the wrong direction for many, many years. And admitting that, feels like committing suicide. Only a few of the economists, psychiatrists and politicians can see through the mist, and have a harmonic ego that can withstand this turmoil. We need more people like that...".

Deniesa now really feels like dark clouds are all around her. Like the dark clouds of Mordor en darking Gondor, the city of the men in the Lord of the Rings Tale. She finds it difficult to breath.

Wondering.

"Is Iwanjka such a negative thinker?". She Observes him

closely. He is strumming his guitar in a happy fashion. "Hmmmm, no he does not seem to be negative". She thinks about the small cities in America, where their taxes go directly to the banks. She thinks about rising taxes and strange new tax constructions in her own city: it seems that the government is squeezing the life out of people in every possible way. She thinks about the government's debts which almost doubled in the past few years. "Hey, she thinks, the taxes I pay are mainly needed to pay our governments debts". "I do not feel this is my debt, I didn't want this. I do not want this system!

"The main reason for this whole mess is the continuously growing debt balloon, and nothing is going to stop this". Then she realises that the system has a monopoly on many things.. "That is strange, economists say there should be 'competition', or at least an alternative. They make organisations compete, but they do not create or allow a system competing with there own economic system, so people can make their own choices. Sounds hypocritical... I want to be able to join a system without debt! I do not care that 'economic progress' is a little slower. I do care for the fact that now we're sitting on an economic atomic bomb!"

"And our governments, our state participates in this whole conspiracy . They serve the big banks. They do not allow nother currencies.". All kinds of conspiracy theories she reads about come up in her mind. But then, looking back on what she learned, she notes that the principles of the banking industry, combined with how people work nowadays are enough to make it all feel like a conspiracy. Just a matter of system dynamics.

"Yuk!", she thinks. I don't want to live in a world like this. "I want a different system!". She decides that she will not sit and wait, now she finally understands how it works. "First, she thinks, let's write it all down". Than I am going to find people who would like to join me. To design, and than implement this new system. We can change this world, why not?

And so it happened, that in that small country called the Netherlands, Deniesa awoke. Deniesa standing for a new society. In Dutch: "DE NIEuwe SAmenleving". And Deniesa soon transformed into a global movement called 'Novaglobe'.... and this book is about exactly that. Deniesa is looking for organisations and people, all over the world, who have a similar wish. To create a new system, create a new world.

4 Part I – Analysis and Synthesis

This part of the book is about looking at today's world. It is about recognising the good partsising as well as the 'the bad' ones, and to find out where we see opportunities for chance and make this world more beautiful.

First, let us take a closer look at most important things you and I see around us. And when we see things we do not like, we should ask ourselves: 'why is that...?' until we understand what is the underlying mechanism. We want to understand the underlying mechanisms, without understanding the mechanisms, we cannot design another system.

The basis of it all: goodness defined.

> "The roots of all ***goodness*** lie in the soil of appreciation for ***goodness***." *Dalai Lama*
>
> When Moses prayed, "show me Thy glory!" God told him "I Myself will make all of My **goodness** pass before you" [Exo 33:18,19]

I first wanted to place this part 'the essence of goodness' in the 'design' part. Then I felt that actually the presented essence of goodness is not new. It is only a synthesis of the existing religious books and Buddhism. It is only a 'normalisation' of all the pages already written. Therefore, I put this -very important- section in the 'Analysis and synthesis part'.

The Seven Principles of Reason

Back to reason. In order to be able to say whether a 'plan' is good, behaviour is 'good', we need a more clear definition of goodness. It is interesting to take notice of how often we use the words 'good' or 'bad' as a qualification of something, without knowing what our basic values are are for this qualification. And we are not alone in this. Politicians, bank directors, directors of multinationals do the same.

In the present society, and especially in the Iconomy 'good' seems to be defined as 'a way to gain more money, material or power'. And bad is the opposite: when something is 'bad' it costs us money, or we loose something.

I began to notice that I find this strange.

> *"More money, consumption and material have become a leading definition of goodness"*

A nice thing to do: ask you relatives, friends or somebody you meet by coincidence on how he or she should define goodness in three sentences. The first thing I observed is that people needed to think about it. The whole idea of goodness was not present in their 'cognitive' system. The second thing I observed is that I got lots of different answers, and that often people couldn't give a practical definition. Thirdly I observed that quite often people came to words as used in the Ten Commandments 'do not lie, do not steal, respect, etc.'.

And I noticed that when the definition of goodness is not real common sense, discussions and debates become pretty useless. That is what is happening in the Netherlands for example. A politician called 'Wilders' states that 'Freedom of speech' is 'very important', and that is his excuseto claim the freedom to say all kinds of things, especially about the Islamic world.

Society and otherpoliticians are not able to give an answer to this claim. And the reason behind it, is that our own basic values are not clearly and simply defined. For me respect is all about freedom of speak. You are free to say things as long as you don't hurt or intrude in somebody else's life, without the need for it.

And that is the case with Geert Wilders. Wilders generalises by saying -implicitly or directly- that the whole Islamic world is criminal. Why say it in such way? Why not say that there are *aspects* in the Islamic world which are not good, in line with his ideas of goodness? Stating it in this way, the door would open for dialogue with people within the Islamic world to exchange visions on goodness, and / or basic values. And find connection points. Make a common sense document. And then use this common sense to talk about *behaviour,* structures, thinking, etc. This would always be at the basis, and apply to every 'religion'. This makes sense.

And then it will prove that regardless of ones ethnic background there are people with good behaviour and bad behaviour...

One more episode from our leading character, Deniesa:

So... Deniesa dives in the big books. She reads Plato, she works her way through the Bible, and a whole pile of Buddhist books. And she asks her Islamic friend about how goodness is defined in the Koran...

And she listens to her heart... her feeling. What feels good?

Soon, she discovers that within all the religions, there is a similar feeling about what it is all about. And even Confucius and Buddha seemed to want to express the same thing. But... how to write downon paper what this thing is?

"Don't lie, don't steal.. don't do to somebody else what you wouldnot want to happen to you, she heard as an echo in her head."

"Hey, she thought, weren't those the Ten Command-ments"? She grabs a bible, and starts to search. "Where on earth can I find the Ten Commandments?, they are not named in the table of contents, strange...". After half an hour of searching and with some help she finds them.

She reads the words... The chapter begins with a quite some threatening words. And the word "commandment" she doesn't like that much either. Sounds pretty intrusive.

Earlier she already sort of decided that "Life and work in unpressed commitment" should be one of the credo's. She read this sentence in a book called "The Heart of Buddha's Learning", a book of Thich Nhat Hanh. And a 'commandment' does not really sound like 'unpressed'.

After some wondering, she decides that once it was probably about the 'Ten Words', of Mozes. In Dutch a word is called 'woord' and sounds like 'waarde' which is Dutch for 'value' (virtue). So hmmm, maybe the ten words once where the same as 'values'. Or recommendations and not 'orders'.

This way of viewing it makes her more happy about the 'Ten commandments'.

Than a song comes around in her inner vision 'Respect yourself', wasn't it Madonna singing that one? And she has some friends 'Bob Marley' type of people, saying always 'Respect' when they greet each other.

"Hmmm, that word comes around pretty often in her life...". She than realises that when you respect the goods from somebody, that you do not steal from them. And that when you respect somebody, you don't lie to that person. And that you certainly do not do things to a person, you respect, which you won't want to be done to you...

"Hey, she thinks... with that only word we express it all... nice!"

"It would be great", she thinks, "that the value base, I am gonna write down, can be shared as a common base by all religions". Because, then, they don't have to fight and argue anymore... it would be great when these words would be commons sense. Hopefully, because Mozes words are the basis, they can share them... She starts to write..."

Listening to the songs of Madonna, heaven comes a long... Like 'Heaven forbid' in the 'Beautiful Stranger Song'. Heaven... What is 'written' in the word 'Heaven', she thinks? Deniesa always puzzles with words... Heaven... Heav'n... Hmmmm... 'Have Non'?

That is a beautiful translation of the word 'Heaven'. Heaven on earth is 'Have Nothing' on earth. This fits perfectly in the feeling she has about possession and the Imagine song of John Lennon: "Imagine no possession". That is similar to "Have Non".... and no pressure (*have to do*). That fits perfectly in Goodvalue no 6 (floating, see further on), based on the Buddhist learnings and they way artists come tot their creations.

"OK, this will be difficult in the West, but we can at least try to make a step in that direction.... and live the 'Modesty' value in a more true manner.". She thinks about the Zeitgeist movie and how it is depicted clearly that the money and economy system (combined called Iconomy by her friend Iwanjka), create our desire for possession and insane consumption and production... "If we could share more... or products are really made to last... or it would cost more money to by a new product than to repair it... this would be more like heaven... she recalls that the Venus project is talking about this to. But how to implement this in the Western world?...".

4.1 The Goodvalues or Seven Principles of Reason

Respect is the basis. As a second 'layer' is she writes:

1. **Oness**. God is the higher harmonism. You are part of god too. We and god are ONE. Deniesa got this one inspired on the 'one' song of U2... you can also call God 'Thing', or 'Goodthing'...
2. **Reciprocity**. Do not to others what you would not like them to do to you. We are equal. This goes for all living things.
3. **Transparency**. Do not lie. Be fully transparent

unless. Let your true colors shine trough.

4. **Modesty**. Do not take more than needed. Give away what you do not need.
5. **Live-and-let-live**. Do what you want want to do, but hurt none unreasonably.
6. **Floating**. Live and work in unpressed commitment. Want instead of must.
7. **Essence**. Do NEVER use more than 333 words to describe the Essence of the GoodValues.

Heaven is about 'have non': No pression, no obligations. And as less possession as possible (material, but it goes for people as well 'have a man or woman'). Freedom for all. Intention instead of promises. Things are done on intention and intrinsic motivation instead of responsibility. Or better: *you* give a *response* based on reason instead of rules and dogmas.

Accepted change at 13 August Novaglobe symposium, Daniel Roos proposed to use 333 words as the delimiter wordcount instead of 337. As being a more holy number...

Proposed add on at 13 August Novaglobe symposium: Daniel Roos and Iwanjka proposed to take a (certain) Sufi approach for the 'second' layer of 'goodness' or 'belief' description: don't use words, but use music.

In a figure this looks like this:

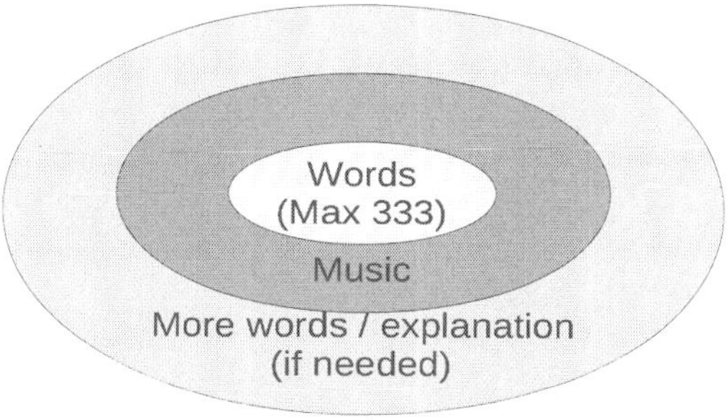

The idea behind the 'Sufi[4]' way is that a 'god' (or 'thing') expression or 'belief' cannot be expressed via a 'mind' or rational way. In the same manner as that you cannot express feelings with words. Our idea is to assemble music from all over the world and put these in a sort of library.

And additional idea is that this 'sound barrier' protects scope creep (Fallacy Syndrome, see the appendix on Misery Creating Syndromes). Of course people and books can add words on how to live the goodvalues, but those words will not make part of the 'essence' description (circle in the middle).

An issue to be decided upon is whether the music may use words... it sounds logical not to do that. And it might be a good idea to do some research on how the Sufi community 'practices' this (note: it is to be expected that with 'Sufi' all kinds of variations exist).

In a next symposium we will elaborate further on this.

---

[4] See the wikipedia on Suffism [Link]

The beauty of this goodvalue definition is that, in essence, it describes -or intends to describe- the essence of the three major world religions: Christianity, Islam and Judaism. And it also harmonises with the essence of Buddhism. The three major religions all belief in Mozes. They start to argue on other topics. Maybe for once focus on similarities in religions instead of differences?

And in fact, our law system, or better our 'justice' system, is based on the same values. "Deniesa is wondering... why is it, in fact that Church and Government did divide? Could it be that the system, Iconomy, itself profits from this division in the same manner as that it profits from dividing people into political parties, so that the van battle each other, while certain persons or the system itself can prevail? Like the gladiators did for Ceasar? "Give the people bread and plays...".

To create a mist for the people to see that in fact they all desire for the same, but cannot see it?...".

Wind of Change - a new orientation

Good. Let is assume that we have consensus, or we can create it, on the definition of the Goodvalues, as describe in the previous chapter. The exact words are irrelevant, the essence is not.

That is a sound soil to sow the seeds of our new society. .

I will first take a look at some important current orientations in our society. And discuss whether I think they are logically, given the requirements of Novaglobe. These orientations are (the proposed new orientation is listed as well):

	From	To
1	Economic growth	Happiness
2	Competition	Synergy
3	Bricks in the wall	Free, unique people
4	Apathy	Interest
5	Fear	Trust
6	Haste	Rest
7	Locking	Free flow
8	Religion	Sense giving

Economic growth → Happiness

> *The primary leading principle within Novaglobe is a maximum of (sustainable) happiness in harmony with the earth.*

This has a a consequence that the present primary steering factor, economic growth, is not the highest goal anymore. Maybe we become even more happy in a less growing economy, or even a shrinking economy (accounted by current measures like 'gross domestic product' (GDP) sum, etc.). Imagine that is possible to create the same level of wellness with less work. That would -with unchanged salaries- result in a lower GDP. And thus a shrinking economy. But we have more free time. And the same amount of 'services' and 'goods' which we can use. Can you imagine this? Is there a problem with this[5]?

I think we can establish this...

And maybe, when we take a really reasonable look into our economic system, we discover that it *has* to shrink to create a more desired system.

I think so.

But this is not a problem.

This could be reasonable good.

In the coming chapters I also will elaborate why the current economic and public (government) cannot deal with happiness as a primary guidance factor instead of economic growth. This leading to the insight that the fundamentals under 'economy' and 'government' are wanted to change. I call these fundamentals 'The Primary Iconomy Constructors (PIC)).

4.2 Competition→ Synergence

Economist state that competition is good and necessary for our welfare. I come more and more to see, that there is a

---

[5]Economists will claim that there is a problem with this, that we should have say an unemployment rate of about 4% at maximum. But this is based on the 'need' for economic growth, not for the need of maintaining happiness or living in harmony with the earth. So what economist claim is not based on reason from another viewpoint...

part they don't see or don't want to see. I call it the 'Hidden Loss Gap'. Of course I agree that it is a good thing that we have innovation, and that people come into action to produce required goods and services. But isn't there another way to provide for that? A more beautiful way? Nowadays economy takes a hight toll. And, as I will make clear further on, it is not so efficient as economist want to make us think.

It is even the other way around: we get a higher and higher *potential efficiency*, but this potential is ruined by Iconomic principles and thinkings. I was happily surprised that I saw that the creators of the Zeitgeist movie came to the same conclusion. A nice example of synchronity, or in another view: if two people at different places in the world, come to the same conclusion or hypothesis, it makes the chance bigger that it is right. Within the Zeitgeist movie the present economic implementation is also called 'anti economy'...

The hidden dark side of competition

After working 10 years in the 'business world' a came to notice that within and between companies a lot of energy goes to breaking each other. It is about the challenge within a company to achieve the most wanted (read: best paid) positions or, when things go not so well, to hold ones job. People almost do anything for this. But it is also about, and that is where this section primary about, the fighting mode *between* companies. When one company wants to grow another company had to shrink. Simple as that. And growth is the only modus companies know. Like cancers igniting growing and exploding. Like firework. Like bombs. Or of course the total market has to grow, but the world market has its limits (which is enlarged by *creating* demand and by *creating* waste)...

I can see the generals (directors). I can see the trenches. I can see the soldiers (employees) who are sent to the front.

They will pay with their lives is they must. They will bleed. The director (general) takes care not to get blood on the hands... but his soul has a lot of blood attached to it. Badkarma.

When one company wants to grow, the other must die, or decrease. Or, the total 'economy' must grow, but this growth cannot take up with the growth greediness of -especially stock market notation- companies.

I came to realise that easily about one third of each company is completely dedicated to how to demolish other companies. Economist state this is required to keep innovation and efficiency at a good level. I think that let say 70 years ago, the capitalistic system was the best system possible at that moment. With the dynamics, information communication and consciousness of people of that time. We just came from state forms like having kings and dictators and so, remember that too.

And I can believe the present economic system has given enormous improvements in technology and society. At this moment it is interesting to note that with the Zeitgeist Moving forward movie, it is stated that this progress has little the to do with the capitalistic model. In the movie it is stated that the progress has been caused by science. I don't know. What I do feel and I agree on this with Jacque Fresco (founder of the Venus Project), that the capitalistic system is far over the top. And, as depicted in chapter on Primary Iconomy Constructors it causes for a high and increasing degree of inefficiency. The hidden loss gap, easily can have already taken bigger proportions than the 'hidden unemployment' in communistic countries. But this hidden loss gap is filled with creating useless jobs and work. So economists and politicians can keep us (and themselves!) in the illusion that the capitalistic-governmental model we have nowadays functions brightly.

It does not.

But, I do not want to 'fight' the present system. We all have came this far on our combined path. The 'system' had brought us material prosperity (at least in the West). But at the other hand it brought us I think spiritual poverty and depletion in the West, and material depletion of the 'poor countries' and earth.

The thing I want to focus on us the bright *chance* which lies in front of us. A far better system became possible. First a more closer look at what a the competition based system has as side effects. And than I want to move on to a very important ingredient a new system: *synergence* instead of *competition.*

I. Competition based <u>inefficiency</u>

The capitalistic system creates a huge amount of hidden loss. After working 10 years at banks, and doing about 1 year research on the money function and creating a 'Good Bank', I came to realise that with about 200 people (100 focus ICT, 100 focus organisationsation) 'I' could create a bank for the whole Netherlands. This bank would offer the fundamental function of a bank: taking care of a currency in a robust and trustful manner. In the Netherlands I guess more than 100.000 people are required to offer the function 'Bank' to society. The main difference with the bank I see, is that the bank function is divided over about 10 competing banks, and that banks started to create all kind of side products. Which had nothing to do with the core business.

Like offering derivate products, mortgages, etc. Products which - to my opinion- do not really offer added values to society, and as we already have seen and will see more, create devastation instead. So why dot it? So, the essence is: with 200 people I have the hypothesis we can create a bank which offer the same added value to society, where we need now say 100.000 people for. That gives a hidden loss gap of more than 99%. Sounds magically, no? You can call me a dreamer, I challenge you to have a dialogue with me on this topic, or write down a 'proof' that my argumentation does not makes sense...

And why did all those in fact unnecessary financial product arise? Because banks wanted to outperform each other. Attract each other clients, etc. Not because the product where really good for society or the human (take a look at the product 'mortgage'). It is a *created demand.*

About false wisdom (for me it is about what classical economists, bankers and politicians want us to belief and, regretfully belief in themselves, deluded by illusion)...

Figure: Delusion of False wisdom... the false wisdom is our present system. (Thanks to Nadine for sending this picture).

II. Capitalism creates huge destruction

Take a look at Hedge funds. These funds are merely based in taking position in derivate financial products. I will not elaborate further on this here. You can take a close look in this subject by searching in the Wikipedia on the words 'hedge fund' or 'derivative product', or 'call and put options' (for instance). These funds do anything for creating money out of money. Here too, watch the Zeitgeist movie for a more profound understanding, the movie gives an excellent analysis how the money system works.

These funds 'shoot' with billions of dollars of capital. They can buy whole companies. And often have a strategy of buying a company, which has taken tens of years to grow. Than split it up, reorganise it, squeeze it, and sell the parts. This 'money wringing' is their business. They do not give a damn of the people working at those companies. They do not give a damn about the consequence of replacing a company towards a country which has the nicest conditions on 'environmental protections', read: spoiling nature. Profit is the only thing counting.

I myself was I witness of the game: ABN AMRO bank was bought by a consortium of Royal Bank of Scotland and Fortis. I worked in the heart of ABN AMRO. I noticed the insane projects being started by the boards. I noticed the hundreds of millions of euro's dropped into the ravines for integration costs. I was witness of the lies the boards told to investors at the stock market about 'synergy profits rocketing the sky' within say three years after the union. We, people working at he floor, *knew* these claims where impossible. Were lies. We *new* it was impossible to -for instance- integrate the hundreds of ICT systems spaced over the bank organisationsations. We *knew* it was not possible to integrate the complex products and processes.

And we told our managers, day after day, in about hundred

memo's, reports, meetings, etc.

But as these kind of organisationsations work: this message does not find its way to the board, or they ignore it. They forced us to continue.. like soldier at the front. Mercy less and sense less. They *could* now. They *should* know. If they were respons-able... Which they are not. These people are not capable of leading banks in a senseful manner...

I myself hit the floor mentally in that period in 2008. I myself had taken a mortgage (how stupid I was then, like many will say once). And combined with the tumult at my 'work', the insane projects (I was spanned between the people doing the job and 'executive management'), a brook down. And because of the mortgage I had taken myself, I even could not leave that toxic environment.

So, I know the devastation this extreme capitalism gives.

And the end of the story of the previous example? The 'consortium' 'Bank of Scotland - Fortis - ABN AMRO' went bankrupt and the governments of Belgium, the Netherlands and England had to buy the stocks, add billions of euro's to keep the balance sheets solvable and give billions of 'guarantees' (which many people around me are not aware of). In the Netherlands now the cycle is closed. ABN AMRO once started as a 'capitalistic' organisation is now a government institution. The serpent has eaten its tale. The **B usiness** and **g O vernment** collided. Became one.

And still our leader belief in the delusion of our system. Gerrit Zalm, once a minister of Finance, than a board member of the DSB bank, and thus accountable for the corrupt thinks this bank is (was, it went bankrupt), now is the CEO of ABN AMRO Bank. How insane.

Anyway, this man dears to state that we can sell ABN AMRO again to the market, at the same price the government bought it once. I think the Dutch society will pay a high price for our blinded and idiotic entrepreneurship of our politicians To my feeling some people at the government found it far too interesting to play for hero and business men. A chance they did not want to let go.... Hopefully we will learn, and at least git the bank as soon as possible from the balance sheets of the Netherland state....

And what happened to Wouter Bos, the minister of Finance accountable for the state buying ABN AMRO bank? He left the sinking ship, saying that he needed more time for his family. Could be true, but timing is suspicious. He now works for one of the biggest consultancy firms in the Netherlands, KPMG. The same goes for Jan Peter Balkenende, the Minister President of the Netherlands at the time of this debacle. He now is partner at Ernst & Young. These consultancy firms are the same firms which hire consultants for about 300 euro's an hour to the government.

So, the 'free market[6]' is killing our ecology. Toxicating it. Or, as the Zeitgeist producer Peter Joseph, states it correctly: in fact our system creates an *anti-economy*, an equivalent for what I call Iconomy.

And than, I do not mention the examples which Deniesa saw in the USA of villages where citizens paid tax which go totally to banks as interest on debts of the city. The whole debt balloon which is integrally connected wiht derivative products (investment funds) and banks. Notice that the huge transactions of buying complete companies is nearly always funded by lending money, and thus inflating the global debtballoon.

I hope, when you read all this, and having probably a sick feeling in the stomach, and thinking about stopping reading this book, you also want to take notice of the following:

---

6 I am not an opponent of the free market. I believe in a free market. But I don't belief in the iconomy. The flowconomy is also a free market, well even more free than the iconomy. But I believe it has a far less destructive potential.

1. We *can* create another form of economy (which I call Flowconomy), in which 'business' (production activities and so) is organised in foundations. Instead of stock market companies. This is a practical step which we now, already can make. We need no new rules to implement it, or politicians frustrating it, etc. And... especially, what *you* can do, as the blood of the system: *you* can decide to buy your goods only at suppliers which have the *foundation form* as a basis. When we all do this, we make the change already. Hedge funds will leave the show...

2. We *can* create a currency which has no intrinsic debt balloon and inflation in it. See ht chapter on the chivi currency. And what *you* can do to help the 'bad' banks go, is to stop lending and taking debt. You *feed* the system when you take a debt. When you buy on credit. When you buy a house with a mortgage. If *you* want, *you* can change this world. Easily...

3. About a good side effect: Technological progress, giving the foundation for a new system...

Technological progress has given us the instruments to do it differently. Technology already has given us the opportunity to do certain processes with far less man hours. And it creates the possibility for us to make far better use of our combined talents. The Internet helps us to realise our common global talent base, wisdom *and* conscious.

Wauw!

Especially it makes possible to be far more place independent. The operating system Linux has been developed by people living in probably all countries. The same goes for the Wikipedia. Brilliant examples of the *good* side of technology. The same technology makes the previous examples possible:

hedge funds could not exist without ICT. The same goes for banks as we know them and all those foolish derivative products. I see these examples as the destructive side, which we should not re-implement in Novaglobe.

I see Linux and the Wikipedia as the constructive side. Both are examples of global cooperation. Without the elements of the Iconomy it. These examples show us the way to Novaglobe. A way out of the devastation nowadays occurring.

The open source world and global cooperation, 'global functions' form the basis for the design of the Flowconomy eco sub function. So, we can make the shift from competition to synergy. To cooperation. To efficiency. From ego-ism and Idiotery (bank bonuses, hedged funds, corruption, debt balloon) to a we-conomy and harmony. Towards reason and modesty.

The age of Milton Friedman, Keynes and other capitalistic driving economists is over then...

"Live simply, so others may simply live!"

[Mahathma Ghandi]

So my main conclusion:

We put so many people to work, and stress them so much, for goods and services which can be produced with so many less hours and stress? In this section I already unveiled some base elements of why our system tends to this. I will give a more fundamental analysis in the chapter on 'Primary Iconomy Constructors '.

4.3 Bricks in the wall → Free and colorful people

This section is about a vision that people should be as free as possible. And that we think that we are free in western society, but we are not. The inverted American dream is becoming true in western society. We are bound by debt. Bound by dogma's. Bound by the companies we work for. Bound by the houses we live in. Are we free?

I believe people should be free as possible to change or move. You are not *forced* to change. You are *free* to change. If a element in the system blocks you, it could be that the system is not facilitating freedom in a sound manner.

I believe that the freedom of people is counter proportional with the sise and penetration of 'the system' in our society.

"All you are, is another brick in the wall", Pink Floyd sings.

And joyfully we all sing along. Thinking *we* are not the bricks in the wall. The *others* are the bricks in the wall. The *losers* are the bricks the wall, the idiots. Not us, them!

Well, let me help me out of your dream: we are.

Only recently it was, I became to really *see* myself as a brick, in a big wall. Jammed between all those other people. Only a thin layer of cement separating us. Take a look at endless apartments glued to each other. Staples of people stacked on each other in flats. And if they were able to move easily, but they are not. Bound by mortgages, regulations and (payable housing market shortage[7]).

---

[7] In the Netherlands there is abundance of place to build new houses. And for tens of thousands people empty office buildings exist. But it is not for the sake for the Iconomy to bring this to the people. Another (logical) effect of our economy implementation. As long as the Primary Iconomy Constructors remain (more on that later), this will not change.

Our living space is becoming more and more less on a daily base. This is true for our geographical space, but it is especially true for our mental space. Our spiritual space. And we just sit and watch how the system squeezes us further and further. Like some chickens some now and than we make some indignant sounds, look at each other, and do...

Nothing.

Was mid '60's one working person per family enough to keep it running, now need two. Mother *and* father. The system wants them both. And we have to work longer and longer (in the Netherlands retirements age is being increased). And with less rest. And with more stress.

> "Our leaders want us to work hard.
> Till your sixtie, seventy, eighty, ninetie years old, till you are dead and gone!"
> [Systemjam song, Iwanjka]

And I see more and more things and fuzz in peoples live. Are you able to get your stuff and leave tomorrow to another country?

This is a question I ask myself frequently to 'asses' my level of freedom or to count the 'sticky spiderweb cords' at my ankles:

Make a list of things to take care of or which withhold you to leave to another country at once, and you know your 'jamlevel': you need to sell a house first? And repay debts because the house is not enough to settle your mortgage debt? You are sealed in a career which you cannot break because if you go, other will jump in your place? You have a business going which you cannot transfer to others? You have children which need to continue to go to schools where they reside now? Your family won't let you go? And probably the worst: you are so attached to your luxury life, the money and material, that you need to create an adequate income?

How free are you?

Think about the "This is the life" song by Amy Mac Donald...

And what about retirement contracts which cannot be broken during the line, assurances which do not allow you to leave, state regulations which do not allow you to leave, tax things, your stock market portfolio which needs daily attention? I have been there myself. All of these things. I know, I know...

Ballast.

And than, I am not yet talking about the uniformity which the system wants us to become. Each person which does not walk along the line is not pleasant for the system. And people thinking for themselves are really a pain in the ass. Maybe the present system is worse on this aspect than the communism... in those countries people probable were *aware* that they were being pushed into a system, into a grid, into a uniform.

In the western countries we are being put in a grid, without noticing it. We live in a delusion. It begins at our schools, our education. And it never ends. The television makes consumers out of us. Tells us to buy a house, get married, get a carreer. Tell, sell, buy. Married with children. And if we are not watchful we tell our friends to do so too. Until we realise what happens, and than we are already to deep in it to see it. We have forgotten the dreams we had as a child. The freedom.

I have seen thousands of men wearing the same grey suits at the banks I worked for. They all looked the same. Wearing a tie. Entering the machine. I saw little compassion in the eyes, I saw little expression. Did those people wear a suite because they wanted to wear it? Or where they slave of the system?

I have been slave of the system for more than ten years. Now I know, I cannot go back. I think and feel.

Again, the word 'sense' comes back. In Dutch we have the word 'zin', meaning something between 'sense' and 'reason'. The reason you do something. Strange that the word 'zin' sounds like 'sin' in English. In Dutch we have the word 'zingeving', freely translated it would make 'sensegiving' in English. The reason why you do things.

You ask your self, those it really make sense, the things I do? Do they relate to the reason why I am on earth. Do they relate to the things I believe in? (values). Do I enjoy my job?

If not, I came to realise that probably the 'process' you are making part of probably does not make sense to the society. Or is not properly organised. It can be because the company you work for has only a money raising goal (like hedge funds), or has a stock notation and is a monopoly entity in the hands of money makers. But, this is another subject, for a later chapter.

Back to sense giving: do you give sense to the world? Do you give sense to your desire and vocale?

Is it your choose to do what you do, or is the system forcing you?

In the earlier days the -more dogmatic- Church made is behave in protocols it created to keep people afraid of -and obeying to- the church (sytem). Now we have gotten ourselves rid of the bad sides of the Church, but we put ourselves under a new religion. Called 'Money', as the Zeitgeist movie states it, or at least, Money is an important component. I call this religion 'Iconomy'.

See the section on 'Primary Iconomy Constructors (PIC)' for a explanation on how this religion works, and keeps us obeying it.

4.4 Apathy → Interest

I see more and more people becoming apathetic. They don't care anymore about what is happening in this world, or what happens with somebody else just living in the same arena. They don't care. And there are many reasons for this. In only name the -to my opinion- most important ones:

1. **Pressure, busy**. We all have so much things to do. Busy. And it seems that in in the USA it is even worse than in the Netherlands. People having multiple jobs next to each other to earn money. This too already begins at school. Children which have to follow lessons for many hours, be afraid for 'at random tests', then do homework for the next day. And at least 'have' one or two 'hobbies' (go to hockey, learn to play piano). In a pressed manner. And visit a young family with children. Ask them if they can do something additionally for society. No time. I feel that people with children nowadays step outside society until their children are self sufficient... Running, running, running...
2. **Lost confidence**. We lost the confidence in the system for the greater part. We lost faith in politicians, our managers and our leaders. And I only can say: with reason. The good people suffer on behave of the bad people. World upside down. And our perspective is decreasing at a daily basis. Things only seem to go worse.
3. **Fear**. An example. Some weeks ago I heard noise at the square in Amersfoort I live above. Youngsters making noise. They had the 'looks of foreigners'. I

thought: "I should say something to them". I didn't. I was afraid. So I called the police. Anonymous. Maybe they didn't know they were causing problems. This is the evil in our society. Not especially the youngsters, but the fear that people don't dear to express themselves directly to the neighbors. And of course, this is exactly what the system likes. In such way it can grow because we 'need' more police man, call centers, camera's, etc. Big money, big GDP growth. But our society... well can we actually still call it a (cohesive) society? A social ecology? A clear systemjam example. How the system dynamics makes the system putting a wall between people. Can we 'blame' the system for this? Well a part of the system is that it does not make it logical that people who have a social cohesion flock with each other. It frustrates this even. So yes, the system is a root cause for the systemjam on this point. More on this in the chapter on the 'togetherhood', which is the name of one of the seven Novaglobe eco sub functions.

4.5 Fear → Trust

This topic is connected to the above described subject. We are being made afraid of live itself. The song 'Living in fear', by Lenny Kravitz pops into my mind:

"I smell the fear that rains inside
The thought of children who must oblige
To tainted dreams and polluted seas
The missing moon and melting trees
A mist of doom and clouds of pain
A toxic waste and an acid rain
The passing of our ignorance
A lifetime spent in abstinence

I living in fear, I living in fear
I can't tell you no lies
I living in fear, I living in fear

Conditioned to hate and them to blame
Their search for God is just the same
Machines for hearts, how warped a view
Forgetting that they're human too
Waiting like a branded steer
Who first will launch the burning spear
When every day may be your last
You think we'd learn from our past"

[Lenny Kravitz, Fear]

And our fear is the Oxygen of the Iconomy. It feeds the blood of the Iconomy. We are chased by all those organisation who want something from us. Tax agencies, banks, governments, schools. I often notice one half of the people in the land I am living is chasing the other ones. And the next day roles change. But everybody is chasing, so it seems. And if organisations are not chasing people it is the people itself: former couples battling each other for years after they split up. Often via the children. Children at schools bullying each other. This is not a good world... this is a evil world, well no, the world is not evil, there is much no-good behaviour. We can change in a split second. Just belief. Be-good. Be lief. Be senseful.

We are made afraid of all the risks that might occur. A child is not allowed to climb a tree anymore. I was raised in Africa. I played in African mud. I guess I enjoyed it. And when I see where nowadays parents are afraid of, regarding their kids. It is not even 10% of the 'risk' I went through as a kid. I climbed the highest trees back in the Netherlands. Feeling the tree moving in the wind. Enjoying the view. Feeling one with nature. I haven't seen a single kid climbing a tree for years now. It is even worse, I think our local government is cutting of the tree branches in order to avoid that children climb the trees.

So, as a child we are blocked to play. The only thing we hear is 'watch out'. And 'you are not allowed' or 'sit quite'. Or children are locked up in their boxes or buggies. Parents afraid that the clothes of the child might get 'dirty', when they shuffle around on the ground. Come on, sense!

Back to the big companies. Think about the insurance companies: "Do you know what can happen, if... you really should...". Are these companies really concerned about are well doing? No, not at all. Nothing. They just want your money. And even worse, the more we create a society in which 'bad things can occur' the bigger their gains. So, what do we end up with? A dangerous feeling society. Iconomy, thanx. It is just a matter of time and system dynamics logic, and a society as we live in now will be created. It is all logically explainable.

The same goes for the various created illnesses. Mexican flu? Right... big pharma profits. We make a pill and create the illness. There are marketing agencies which are specialised in creating 'demand' for a certain 'medicin'. Did you know that? How evil. Again a direct consequence of the Iconomy. We ask for it, if we let the Iconomy exist.

When I worked for Ordina, a big software company in the Netherlands, I was taught that the first tactic to sell a thing was to make the client scared. Beautiful. Nice for your karma. Selling is lying,. That I know now. And I see it at a daily base on television, bill boards, etc. We are being conditioned, hypnotised each minute of the day. Time to wake up.

Back to the children not allowed to play. The children from now, are the adults later. And when people forget how to play, you are half dead already. You do not feel sense anymore. You fall asleep. But the fear is maybe worse. It freezes us. It creates a high systemjam. An spreading virus of people putting fear in other ones lives. And it is necessary that the other starts to reflect this fear, otherwise you ruin ones pillar of existence. So being differently is not accepted. Or even ruled out. The free people become outcasts...

There is only one certainty in live: uncertainty. And why is that a problem?

4.6 Haste → Rest

Corsica a little island, just between France in Italy, knows a very nice valley.

Called 'Restonica'...

This item I already addressed one time earlier as well. No time, no time. We need to run. Time is money. A famous song in the Netherlands goes like: "Geen tijd, geen tijd, we moeten rennen, springen, vallen en weer opstaan". Freely translated?: "No time, no time, we need to run, jump, fall and stand up again...". It is a song by Herman van Veen.

An interesting side effect of collecting support signatures for our political party New Netherland, just next to the city halls learned me much. I have been watching people for two weeks. And nearly everybody had haste. We plan our days in blocks of 5 minutes. I have seen the pressure at their faces. Tension. Interrupt them in their flow, and they mumble something like that they "Really don't have time".

One of the credo's which entered my mind after my suicide attempt was:

"The Slower you Live the longer it Lasts"

Do you ride the wave of time, or does it ride you? Being on the wave, is a well know Buddhist credo as well. It is about the same.

The 'nice' thing about my suicide attempt is that I really felt reborn. I was granted a new life. I could compare it with the case that I had 'succeeded': why should I rush? In the case I had succeeded, I wouldn't be able to do anything in this world at all. So why rush? Death escaped me. And I had taken distance of all material things like possessions. You cannot take them with you when you die. So, why take a big effort in collecting them?

I really hope that people will be able to get the feeling I had, and still have, after my suicide regarding this aspect. That you don't HAVE to achieve ANYTHING. And that it is only that you WANT to desire maybe EVERYTHING that makes you moving.

I want *a lot* (experience, not possession), but I don' *have to* do anything. And this, I noticed makes the inspiration for work optimal. I realised that an artist will not get the required inspiration when pushed too much. But when there is no desire, no 'wanting' (interesting that a 'want' has to do with magic, with creation) nothing happens either. "You *want* to ride a nice wave, but you enjoy lying in the ocean already". And you *know* a nice wave will always come. Than abundance enters your life. This I learned while wave surfing at Biarritz and Lanzarote.

And some other nice encoded word wisdom:

"Do you die or dye your live?" [Iwanjka]

(And remember the Led Zeppelin song, Stairway to Heaven: sometimes words have two meanings...)

I noticed that 'die' and 'dye' sound the same, but when we use the different meanings it is the complete opposite. When we are pressed the inspiration is blocked. And thus we cannot get inspiration to paint a nice painting for our lives. Thus we start die-ing. Time is a required paint for the painting. And so are the goodvalues to make the paining work. Without floating space we block the cosmos to bring the good thing in our lives which build up a desired reality. Without doing truly good, we block the essence of our 'creamation' power. We 'block' the 'law' of attraction. Well, we will attract bad things. Our life will become worse. By collecting possession and getting stuck in our live (contracts, marry, etc.) we block the floating essence, and thus dye-ing possibilities.

But being able to follow the time instead of the time chasing you is one of the most important ingredients, which we almost completely killed. In Dutch 'time' is 'tijd', which sounds like 'tide'. I came to say, "Just follow the tide"... more and more I came to notice that our life takes place like floating on an ocean. In the same manner as that we use a lot of sound related words. An ocean is also about waves... But following the tide in Western countries is difficult. We try to steer the tide. Manipulate the tide. Manipulate the natural flow of things. We have to be at work at 9AM, we have to bring the kids to school at 8AM, we have to visit a birthday party in the weekend, etc., etc. And I even think a lot off people are addicted to time pressure. They cannot stand the feeling of idleness. It makes them think and feel, look inside. And that is for many, man people very scary... maybe it it raises the desire of a different life they don't live. And instead of examining those feelings we go back to pressure zone and focus on all those 'little things' we really have to do and comply to... Instead of dying a new life we want to live, we die our Selves...

We can learn a lot of Africa I guess. And this country can learn a lot from the West. We can lean about unpressed life. And that we can be happy without chasing things. And 'they' can maybe adapt a little bit of the 'western commitment'. I think blending Africa and the West makes a golden combination... the way to a life in 'unpressed commitment', see the goodvalues.

Think about it....

In Dutch I say: "Onder druk gaat alles stuk", under pressure everything will break. This could be translated with something like: "Press makes a mess"... Press... stress...

4.7 Getting jammed → Flow / possibility to change

It seems to be normal that we dig ourselves in deeper and deeper. How deeper the better. This is not a problem if you stay at the same point (geographical) or if you as a human do not change. At the other hand, if you wanna change your situation you might have to go though a gigantic reorganisation process.

In the Netherlands we introduced indirectly a tax for divorcing. How does it work? Well, about 60% of the households in the Netherlands has a mortgage on their house. Mainly based on two incomes, and pretty at the top of the couple's lending capacity. Couple divorces (at least about 30% of the married people do divorce). This leads often to the situation that the house has to be sold. And this 'transaction' costs 6% tax on the housing price, which makes easily 15.000 euros. And if the prices of houses do not rise -

which seem to be the case nowadays- a new buyer will not pay this tax, so the people leaving the house has to pay for it.

So, changing ones individual live is parasited upon by the state. Or in different words: on more and more life cycle changes, the government moves in to get some money from it. And if is not the government it is the legions of judges, insurance companies, lawyers, etc. Which designed legislation to block your natural flow and make you pay first.

Strange, no? "Divorce tax".

It almost looks like that the church institute created this divorce tax, to force people to stay longer in their marriage...

Change is not wanted. Moving around is not wanted. Change is prohibited, tax-weighed and more an more difficult.

Once we were nomads. Free people. Could change and move whenever you wanted to. We even made the gypsies people exchange their mobiles homes into concrete unmovable houses. Flow has halted.

The Iconomy likes people to be chained by laws. To be predictable. To remain in fear and under pressure. Because in that way they will obey, will not think for themselves, and follow their decrees. And can create maximum money for the Iconomy to grow and maintain itself. The Iconomy is the beast in bible-terms, I tell you...

4.8 Pressure → Sense

At the same moment when I am writing this book, I was reading the book 'Collision, the Catastrophe', by Sarah Morton. She describes in her book impressively how she observed the school system as a child. The pressure. The terror which is put on the children by teachers. Often offcourse without doing this on purpose, I believe. Or the feeling not to want to do the things which are forced on you.

Things which do not fit to your character, talents or desires. In Sarah's case it is about 'special' schools for children which do not fit in the 'normal' school system (in Dutch called 'SO', Special Onderwijs, meaning special school).

The abbreviation 'SO' has a special meaning for me in this context. It is also the name for the 'at random' tests which where put on me and my scholar fellows at my school time. At each minute of the day you had to be on your careful whether a teacher would raise his voice and say: "okay children, remover your books, SO time...". And then you think: "Fuck! I learned all different subjects today, but not this one.... aiiiii". And remember that this gave a constant feeling of distress and an unpleasant state. And some teachers gave me the feeling that they enjoyed their power. And enjoyed our arousal and fear.

This is not the way. I feel and know. We are making our children sick. They will enter their adult days feeling that the world cannot be trust. And probably start trans formating all those years of frustration towards their colleagues they are working with. And of course, 'sicknesses' like ADHD are directly related to this kind of idiot school system. I feel.

I came to see teachers as snipers. Wanting to shoot at me, when I am at my most vulnerable moment...

Sarah Morton gives a insight in her school period as was she giving a report on a war scene. Snipers, defense strategies, pressure, breaking out, trying to recover, counter attack, fighting... sounds like war. An war of emotions. As said earlier: world war three is already going on in our midst...

I see these examples symptomatic for our society. In addition to the fact that these school systems break the will of the child, it results in the very important thing that children are less and less able to *feel* themselves. To feel what they want. In Dutch: "to feel their 'zin'", meaning in English something like 'sense'. And it has to do with being able to determine what makes you happy in life. And what is your vocal in this life. And if you are not able to feel this, it is like being without your compass. And this results in people who feel themselves deprived in this life. Lost.

And, additionally we screw the self learning ability of our children. And maybe the most important: people end up in careers and places where they will not get to be happy. And do not use their talents in an adequate manner for society. Or even get destructive or sick.

Sensegiving has everything to do with where your talent and energy resides at that very moment. And that has a lot to do with emotion and sense. And that on its turn has everything do to with rest and an unpressed state.

In the same manner as that an artist will not come to his inspiration when pressed, a child will not develop its ability to feel its sense in this world. When the child gets pushed constantly and people force it to do all kinds of things which are not part of its natural flow. A next crucial factor for a child to develop is entrepreneurship. And this can only develop if the child is intrinsically motivated for a certain goal and has sufficient freedom (and companionship). For entrepreneurship you need to dare to ask people for help or information. Be assertive. Be curious. Be able to find out what is needed tot fulfill your creation, plan, dream. Be trustful.

This is not a main focus on today's schools .

At the school I was, things like entrepreneurship, think for yourself and giving expression to your inspiration were suppressed. It was a 'religious' school. I have a clear remembrance we had 'poetry' class. We were asked what we read in a certain poem. I gave my vision, feeling and expression. It was wrong, because the teacher had his own (religious) explanation with the poem. In other words: my wisdom was ignored, or even worse: rejected. My 'expression' was wrong, false.

Expression can never be wrong. Can never be 'false', I think. We made thinkings dogmatic, and thus closed our eyes for the beauty of the fantasy and thinkings of others.

I had to follow the rules. Rules will make fools. Fools make rules.

And, of course, we, the adults, are the most important factors in the shaping of the new generation: if *we* are not able to feel where our sense resides, our leads us to. If we go to our work, disliking it, and do not change the situation. What kind of children does this lead to?

A final word... I just come to realise that the architects of the school system are not the teachers anymore. No, it is the government people in the departments plotting how our children should be taught. What kind of people are that? Probably not the ones who really like teaching, in such a case, they would not be sitting at a 'dull' office (probably combined with that their talent is not in teaching(?)). So, teachers at schools see themselves confronted with an idiot teaching system by a group of bureaucrats. And this on its turn destroys their pleasure in work, and this will be transported to the children...

And, as it goes everywhere in the iconomic system: these people (government education department staff) start to create things to capitalise themselves). For example to keep their jobs. They will make up things even if they are not needed, or even worse: will bring badness. In the same manner as Microsoft pushes Windows Vista into the market, to retain profit figures at high levels, these departments just produce a big 'school' system, teaching model. Which needs a lot of government officers to maintain and control it. And the teachers and children, do they profit? No.... that is way I believe that in the new world a highest goal of officers working at the government is to make their function obsolete. Then you really improve the system. But this is not possible in the present system, because again: who is going to pay the rent, the mortgage? And... somebody's position stands for social status. Insane...

4.9 Religion → Sensegiving

Religion is often named in one sentence with sensegiving[8]. But... is religion about sensegiving? About reason? For me, the words 'zin' (dutch for sense), 'zijn' (Dutch for 'to be'), sun, zen and sense are connected. Sensegiving for me has to do with whether you live a life which *makes sense*. Which gives sense to your own life, and / or the life of others. And, as Raoul Schepers states it: are you a giver or taker (consumer). I like giving people around me...

"I want to give, I want to live"

[Neil Young, Miner for a Heart of Gold]

> The words 'zin' (Dutch for sense), 'zijn' (Dutch for being), sun, sense have a high connecting resonance and seem to have a common essence. The word 'sin' sounds like 'zin' and 'sun'. Could it be that the religious institutes gave 'sin' a negative meaning to keep people out of the sun? ("The preacher likes the cold, Californian dreaming song").

So, what is it that makes sense? And sense is highly connected to the word 'reason'. And do you things because 'it should be done like that', or can you explain me, based on common ground values, why it is reasonable to do it? Or can

8 In Dutch there is the word 'Zingeving' (Sense Giving), which is often uses as a more generic term for the collection of say religion, way of life, Buddhism, etc. I couldn't find a proper synonym in English, so I decided to introduce the term in English, because it is such a strong and important word. Sensegiving.

you give me a human explanation, based on intuition and feeling why it should happen? Ratio and Emotion form the basis. The head and the heart. If you connect both, you get spirilogic. And that is our temptation: can we combine head and heart in a reasonable manner?

Actually, religion seems mostly based on rules, and 'dogmas'. I prefer to replace religion by sensegiving. If you are a true believer, and live for example the words of Mozes, your religion and my 'sensegiving' are the same. If you put rules above sense, you do not live sensegiving. I think.

*In the Netherlands about **1 million** people takes anti depressants. Yearly. That makes about 1 out 10 adult inhabitant. 10%. I think that these people not really feel the live a senseful live. High time politics start to examine why so many people do not live a sense full live? Could it be a symptom of a sick society?*

Well, living a more sense full life needs the Iconomy, the present system to leave the show. But Iconomy does not want that... Again, watch Zeitgeist Moving forward movie, and you'll understand, if you not already do understand it.

REM, "Losing My Religion", for me this song is about the wanting for a compassionate fellow world inhabitants. To feel the connection. Inspiration. To see is somebody is inspired, look for the glance in onces eyes. The glance, the twinkling of a being being in once talent, vocale, energy and course. And the soul being close to earth (the eye is the mirror of the sole). If you see misty eyes, no sparkles, you know enough. Why is it, you think, young children have bright eyes? The soul is still close by. Their will is not yet broken. They feel still free to play...

And seeing that the present system, which can be seen as a religion, will not bring us happiness. So we will leave it. It is good it gets lost. The challenge is not to get lost ourselves in this process...

And, of course, the loosing my religion song is about the forced convictions. The conditioning. And it is not only about the 'church', it also about all things which have been told to us to be good or not, but which are in essence not true. Like achieving a career and earning lots of money. Based on the goodvalues, I can not reason why earning a lot of money or working 80 hours a week for retrieving a high position is good. And the song is about the desire to let the delusion go. The come back to our inner selves, our kernels. And to live in a society which carries ourselves and protects is, so that we *can* live our true selves.

Is a society in which children at the age of four stop with playing senseful? Is a society senseful in which people are are tempted or even forced to take loans and become slaves of the banks and their employers?

This system does not seem to make sense to me.

When we erase all, and make a new design? How would it look like? Imagine...

We have forgotten that giving makes happy. How can it be that somebody calls himself a Christian, lives in a villa 'worth' about 1,5 million euro's, and is driving around in a jaguar? As long as people are starving in this world of hunger, or are jammed because of their financial situation, this is not possible. If you do not give, you are not a Christian. It think, feel. "Do not take more than necessary" (modesty remember), or give away what yo don't need. 'Salonchristians' I call these people. They have disillusioned themselves they do good. Again, based on the goodvalues, I cannot agree on their reasoning and way of life.

How come, that people do not give anymore (I pose this charged)? Because of the iconomy... we think that we have a 'system' which takes care of the sick and poor. And that this sets us free from our sense to help people in need personally. I have experienced this, and experience this as one big delusion and camouflage. A nice way to temper our conscious. Now we say: "I already pay enough taxes, I paid my share!". And, than we start looking to the system to to the 'dirty' work. And the system is spoiling the given value in a higher an higher rate. And... because of our endless mortgages we don't feel we can miss money: "first I have to pay of the mortgage"...

I am afraid that what Mozes warned us for, did happen. He said: "Do not make an icon". It happened. The Bible has become an icon, how ironically. This book is one big icon of the essence of god, of goodness. And where too many words moved in, the message gets distorted, or even totally camouflaged. It gets lost in the words. Is it a coincidence that 'bible' sounds like 'bable'? It don't think so. The bible itself became a source of confusement and misunderstanding and conflicts. Don Willard, friend, musician and deeply in history recently told me that the Bible was written one hundred years after Christ died. Did Jezus maybe already feel that goodness and sensegiving should not be written down in a thick book? "The more words are used to bring the message, the more the essence gets lost..."?

This is all logical, when one realises who has written the bible. Did Jesus do it himself? Or are practically all words written by people who had the desire to be like him, or maybe more often, 'have' his power? And to capitalise on his goodness and words, in favor of their own ego's? I think practically no woman has written in this book for example. Which is already a sign on the wall (who are the ones fighting normally? Men. Who are the ones raping? Men... etc.). And when this continuous over and over, year in year out, the whole story evolves in its own way. In the same manner as psychiatrist and pharmaceutic industry evolved the DSM-IV psychiatric models. Driven by power, money and ego. Mainly. Not on sense and feeling.

And our system is a icon. It deludes us from clear seeing. Obscured by clouds we are. We do not see the whole picture anymore. Between us and our neighbor, or the man being helpless on the street is the 'system', the iconomy, which makes it almost impossible for us to remain human. To see the essence of sense and humanity. And about true belief. Be Lief.

I think Jezus knew that he should not write down to much words. Or he wasn't a writer at all. I think he knew too much words would kill his message. Would distract peoples attention from essence to the words used. From true belief towards the icon and peoples own desires and destructive thinkings. And making a thick book would make people reading the book, looking for the meaning, would make them talk about it. Instead of *living* it...

The essence of all world religions is good. See the chapter on goodvalues as well. And read the appendix on the 'Five Syndroms of Misery Creation' to understand how religion (and psychiatry), but law as well, created such thick books, but lost essence.

We can learn so much out of history...

"The way towards Utopia is written in History."

Ιστορία is Greek for 'History'... Looks like Utopia?

5 The impact of Childhood

This chapter has been fully contributed by the Dutch Author and childhood 'expert' Sara Morton. See for more information (in Dutch, you might try using Google Translator or so), her website www.afwijkend-en-toch-zo-gewoon.nl (meaning: different but normal). Note the resonance with the book 'The Normal Personality', by professor Stephen Reiss, which I highly recommend, and which forms the basis for the RdRemedy[9] Sarah is also involved in curing / healing people with 'mental diagnosis'. She is a steering team the Humansound chapter in The Netherlands (one of the seven eco subdomains, see the 'design part' of this book.

From a cluster of cells, one day you will grow into a mature human being. In the very beginning you will have no opinion of your own. The experiences and messages you gather along the way will form their basis. Of course, every human being has its own talents and unique character, but in general this is how human development progresses: at the start of your life, you have no knowledge of anything. Intellectual maturity will be influenced by factors like a person's environment, relationships with others and experiences gained. Intellectual development starts as early as in the womb. The womb is a naturally safe and warm place. Although the little creature rarely receives personal attention, it does not feel lonely. If the mother is frightened or stressed, the foetus will sense this and so, will receive information about the outside world. In case of famine, the foetus will 'learn' something about life too. Its body will be very economical with energy for the rest of its life. This imprint starts earlier than most realise.

---

[9] RdRemedy stands for Reiss-HumanSound Depression Remedy. See www.levensklem.nl for more information. It is a non-psychitraric curing method based healing method for people in a 'severe depression' (mental 'illness'). But more general the method is applicable for healing the most of the DSM-IV diagnosis... DSM IV is the psychiatric system 'diseases' book. English version of the book 'Diagnosis Lifejam' is currently being translated by Liduina Wildenburg, and is expected to be released mid / end 2011.

Once the child is born, the influence of the environment is much stronger. The warm, organic enclosure has disappeared. All sounds and other impressions which were first muted, will now enter in full intensity. The biology of a child is prepared for the transition from the living womb to the partly living outside world. It expects it. In the case of a natural birth, the baby will experience it without emotional trauma and with reasonable equanimity. Of course it will be a shock, an overwhelming event, but the child is able to cope with it. Its whole being expects to end up in its mother's arms, its body against hers. The umbilical cord still pumps oxygenated blood to the newborn baby. Gradually, it will start breathing of its own accord.

What it is not prepared for is the childbirth procedures of most hospitals. The nurse cuts the umbilical cord and the baby has to gasp for oxygen immediately. The sudden presence of dry air hurts its lungs. Often the baby gets a slap on the back to make it cry. Loud crying is a good sign according to nursing staff. The system is based on violence. Then the nursing staff takes the baby away from the mother for a check-up. The physical contact is unloving and cold.

For minutes the baby lays exposed and naked. It can't defend itself. No matter how loud it cries, it can't get out of this situation. It cries like someone suffering excruciating pain. A baby simply cannot understand what is going on. A baby is all need, instinct, sensation. Nature doesn't detect torture, unless it is really taking place. It is really as bad as it sounds.

The earlier in childhood, the deeper the impression. Until the age of three, you have no conscious recollection of your childhood, because your brains have not yet sufficiently matured. The images and thoughts are erased, you cannot understand what happened. Yet, your body has stored all the information. Deeply entrenched patterns and impressions. As an adult, you may suffer from physical and psychological ailments, without knowing where they come from. You will live your life and deal with situations and relationships as you have unconsciously learned. How you grew up is all you remember. That is your point of departure. There is yet another reason why most of us are a product of our childhood. Parents find themselves reacting to their child out of their own childhood wounds, and embodying the same dysfunctional behaviours that their parents passed on to them. This is by no means logical. Usually, you would choose to protect others and safeguard them from the pain you have suffered yourself. And most parents love their children dearly, don't they?

Here it is: Most people are unaware of what happened to them. They have learned to deny their experiences. To admit to themselves the situation is hopeless, that it is not right, yet they are unable to change it, is a heavy psychological blow. So the child will end up believing that what is happening is normal.

With their own life experience as a guide, parents/carers try to erase the child's traumatic experiences from its mind by saying, "It is part of life", "It's for your own good" "It's your own doing" and other remarks like that. The parent/carer presents himself as infallible. He or she is always right, the child is wrong.

As carers (particularly parents) are the child's prime example, the key people who teach children what life is all about, the child can only copy their standards, no matter how rebellious the child appears to be, no matter how hard it resists instinctively.

Most children are raised with social values. Those values teach children for example, how to be nice and what could hurt others. That is completely natural. They learn primarily by example: the behaviour and feelings that people show and the way people deal with each other. To a lesser extent, they learn from what carers/parents say to them.

You could tell a child to be nice and it should not hurt others, but if you yourself smack your child because you want it to listen to you or because you have lost your temper, you teach the child that violence is an acceptable way to resolve conflict.

If, as a (young) child, you learn that you have to fight for your basic needs, you will be prepared to use violence much quicker in later life, than someone who grew up in harmony.

Have you been treated with respect as a child, then you will also treat others with respect. Were you despised on the other hand, you will later have this attitude towards others who rank lower than you.

A baby is accustomed to be with its primary caregivers. First the mother, than the father, than the ever increasing number of familiar group members. In addition to care, feeding, changing, etc., a baby needs constant closeness in order to feel safe, complete and okay. If you leave your baby alone, it will be in a state of emptiness and desire. In the wild it is dangerous for a helpless child to be left alone. Although we have our security reasonably under control, a baby will instinctively sense mortal fear, even in a modern home. It will do its best to get someone's attention. It will cry or scream until it falls asleep, totally exhausted. A baby who has to fend for itself, is like a cripple without a wheelchair.

The arguments for letting a baby cry itself to sleep are that it would otherwise get spoiled or become less independent. Especially in the western world it is customary to keep a child at bay. It should sleep in a separate room. Parents and child are separated, as parents are, for financial reasons, forced to work outdoors. The baby has to stay in a child care facility, where there could be as many as ten babies taken care of by only a couple of minders. Most parents who go out with a baby, use a pram or buggy, pushing the child away from them as opposed to facing them.

Pampering is not what you think, it is pure neglect. The parent/carer is unable to give the child what it really needs, is possibly not even aware of the baby's needs and spoils it with indulgence, and other things children don't need: a pacifier to calm a baby, sweets when a child hurts itself or is upset. Older children are bribed with gifts.

Figure: Zeitgeist Moving Forward, Our children are swiftly introduced in our Iconomy Religion, Have, have, have... Location 1

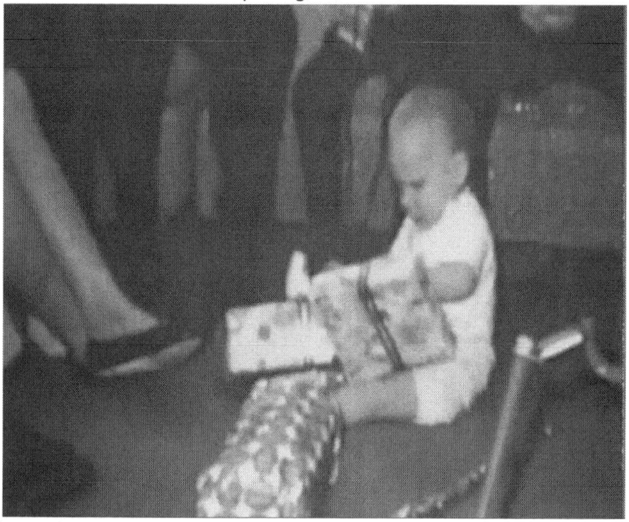

hour, 4 minutes.

Instead of setting an example and lead, parents/carers facilitate the wishes of the child, even if those wishes are unhealthy. For example, the child is allowed to watch television for hours each day and when it whines for sweets or snacks, it gets it. It is merely an empty substitute for what they truly desire. Love and appreciation for who they are. Someone with whom they can share their feelings and experiences. Comforting arms, when scared, sad or in pain. Or just the enjoyment of being noticed. It's not the gifts and goodies that you best remember later. It is the pleasant moments together. The atmosphere. Playing with friends. Snowballs fights, strolling along the beach, bake a cake with mom or dad, play fighting. Then a child will flourish.

A baby monkey spends all day with his mother, closely against her. In the western world, contact between mother and baby consists of feeding, changing, a little play and the occasional hug. Most of time the baby has to wait. This is why the child will not be complete, it will also experience a loss later in life. In a more natural form of life, work and home is not strictly separated. The baby stays close to the mother, against her in a sling. The mother is able to do her own thing. The baby feels connected to life, feels safe.

Although it is not really capable of doing anything, it participates to the activity by watching and listening. It takes in information and gets the life experience it needs to grow into an independent adult. Instead of sitting at home and feeling alone, living from feed to feed, the mother moves in circles where she is most in her element: among peers. She is part of a group. An older child can roam around, play with other children or join the adults. Just like young animals learn. They observe closely, listen and try it themselves. They practice and become more precise.

Children ask for a challenging environment, preferably with lots of nature ready to explore, close by. Running, climbing, hiding, building a hut. Getting acquainted with the elements. But safety and hygiene are now the highest priority. Children are heavier and move around less. Accidents happen just because they don't know their bodies, their motor skills deteriorate and they do not learn to assess risk.

Of course it is our responsibility to protect children from serious danger, but the children of today are no longer allowed to get hurt or even get dirty.

Formal education is not so much about learning, it is more like an adaptation training. Showing own initiative is not appropriate, except in leisure time. As a child, you must wait until the teacher instructs you. You learn to switch on and off. It is mostly paperwork. Many, if not most children do not understand what the point of school is. They are bored or just feel overloaded. Independence is not stimulated. What a child should be able to do is decided up front. Forcing children can have the desired result, but will always cause struggle and stress. Moreover, the stress takes up a large part of the child's mind. The result is that it will then focus less on learning. While of course it is valuable to be able to read, write and count, many children dislike the teaching methods. They are not free to make connections or discover things themselves. The stories and assignments are often meaningless and pre-programmed.

Children are not lazy and unmotivated by nature. They are curious and resourceful. They learn by interaction and by copying adults. For example, reading a story to child, a story he or she thinks is beautiful or exciting, may just inspire the child to learn to read itself, it might learn that books could become an important part of his or her life.

By involving a child in writing a card (eg for grandma's birthday), it could become eager and wanting to learn to write itself, when the time is ripe.

This goes for everything. Lead by example rather than impose the child. In general, children like to be part of a group. Their social nature makes them join others. Every child is different in when they are ready for the next step. If a child is fascinated by something, it takes the information in much quicker. Adults can be amazed by the vast progress a child is able to make and the energy it is willing to put into it.

Sarah Morton

6 On Money

Money is the substance for our value circulation system, and thus a crucial factor in reorganizing our ecosystem. This chapter depicts the history of money (which is for some people well known already), and why it is breaking down, and is no good as it is. If you know already about money evolved, about money creation and debt, you can skip this chapter. Understanding the present money system is however crucial for redesigning our world: if we want it or not, alternative money will be *the* key to create an alternative ecosystem.

Shells

Once, we just exchanged goods. One buffalo skin for a bucket of berries. But... if you do not have the buffalo skin, what do you do than? Than you have to create something that replaces the value of the buffalo skin.

I have been told that shells was one of the earliest 'buffer' instrument for trading. In April you sell your buffalo skin for 10 shells, and in august you buy with seven shells berries you like. You remain three shells for other purposes.

In those days the numbers behind the the dot didn't matter ($1,99?). And intrinsic inflation was another thing which was not invented yet.

But... everybody can find shells, so the value of a shell could decrease rapidly over time. The only way to avoid this, is to agree within the 'shell community', to not add new shells as a currency.

Gold

Soon, gold became to be the primary format as a currency. The reason is not that people liked the appearance, more important: it is scarce. It is not easily to find, create and thus to add to the 'money system'. And it does not deteriorate.

Via this way a sort of global, common 'blood' arose. Gold can be stored, exchanged, accumulated and it remains its value in a reasonable way. An interesting thing: when actually was the name 'money' introduced? Well, never mind, lets call this concept money.

Money is not bad. Money is magic. With the money you earn in your country, you can create a hospital in another country. If you like this to happen. I came to notice that money is a transformation thing. To transform goods, services at one place, at a certain time into other goods, shapes and service at another time at another place. Pure magic. A nice thing to have around...

Martijn Brasem says about money in his book 'Equality Freedom Connectedness', that it is a form of energy. I think this is true.

Money pot

But, through the ages, money has transformed from a utility into into a possession. At thing to gain, aggregate and fight for. Kill for. What once was a minor thing: we needed a transformation thing to change goods, it has become a major thing: we work to get money. Huh?

Money was a trading thing, no?

Times changed.

Banks

Then came the banks. They noticed that carrying around with money is quite a burden, and some people tend to take it away without the owners agreeing on it: they steal it. So additionally it was quite unsafe to have your gold with you in your house.

Than the banks moved in. They started to take care of the collective gold storage.

At the same time the value paper (note) arose: the bank retained the gold for you, and as a 'swap' you got a paper with the amount of money you possessed on it. Actually the paper is a loan from you to the bank, you could get some amount in gold from the bank. So, the banks probably started to be lenders first.

The world has turned around on this subject it seems: now everybody is bound by debt, and the people have lend lots of money from the banks. That is strange...

Well, back to the early banks. Instead of paying with gold, we started to pay with these 'debt notes'. And later these papers where not anymore specific for a name, but generic and were called dollars. In those days you could go to the bank with your dollar and there was gold. How different is it now.

> The phenomenon that banks materially posses exactly the amount of gold for the banknotes floating around is called **'Golden Standard'**. Via this mechanism it is guaranteed that the amount of money remains more or less the same. Important

to note...

Maybe good to mention that this system - when the gold amount was stable - did not know intrinsic inflation, as we have nowadays.

Alas, alas... peoples greediness took over.

Fractional banking - start of money creation

After a while bankers found out that the mass of gold was pretty stable in their depots. In fact society didn't see that gold any more. And economists invented the credo that lending is good for the economy.

Companies, for example, could borrow say $10.000 dollar against say 4% interest per year. And if they where able to make 10% profit on that $10.000 dollar, it was $600 dollars annual profit, out of nothing ($600 = $1.000 profit minus $400 interest)! That is interesting... This is called 'efficient use of production factors'.

In the early days of lending, you could only lend money to somebody, if you really 'had' the money. Say: you have 1.000 dollar, than you can lend somebody else, maximally 1.000 dollars.

And this transaction does not change the total amount of money running around in the money system.

Saying it in different words: if nobody wanted or wasn't able to lend you 1.000 dollars you wouldn't get it.

That changed when economists and bankers decided that banks should be allowed to lend money, which they didn't posses. Now the devil moves in. This concept of course got a difficult and high ending sounding name 'fractional banking'. In fact it is stealing.

Fractional banking is stealing - why?

Imagine that a bank itself has 100.000 dollar. Normally, it would not be allowed to lend more than that 100.000 dollars to others.

Nowadays it is allowed to lend about a tenfold of this.

But... this money does not exist! So... once somebody gets a loan, that amount is being added to the total of money running around, and is being created.

The idea behind it, is that it 'never' occurs that all the people at the same time come and get their money. "So why keep it stored 'unused'?", The smart business men thought.

Example: Imagine a bank maintains for say 10 million dollars in gold. It is allowed to lend for about 3% of it in dollars. So the bank lends 300.000 dollars. Against say 5% interest per year. That is about 15.000 dollar. So the bank pulls 15.000 dollar per year out of the society without adding value to that same society!?

Why is it allowed to do this? That is why I call banks thieves.

And it even gets worse: that 300.000 additional dollar in the system, makes the money in your pocket decrease in value. This is the beginning of what I mention 'intrinsic' inflation.

So, we get stolen at two sides: 1. The bank pulls 15.000 per year out of our society (via interest), 2. It creates 300.000 dollar and making the money in our pockets decrease in a ration of about "new_money divided by money_in_system".

Nice.

Now I know where the marble halls get paid by. Not because the bank adds value to society. Or that the bank people work so hard, or are so clever... or whatever. The banking sector gets money for nothing. But you bleed. Recall that banks easily make about billions profit per year. This is logical because the balance sheets sum up to about hundreds of billions. Takes just a percentage of the amount of created money an presents it as a profits result.

Robin Hood would do a great job to just get dismantle the banks and give the money to society, the money they stole.

But... there is no money left. The vicious circle is that banks have to create new money in order to get the interest-debt cycle running.

Karma lessons

I now understand why I had to work 10 years at banks. Why I, too, expressed time in money. 15 minutes was 25 euro's, because I earned 100 euro's an hour at the bank as an interimmer. So, if I had to choose between buying a second hand cloth for my daughter for 5 euro's and one hour for getting it, or 25 euro's in the shop in not 'wasting time', I choose the latest.

No I try and want to live the inverse. I desire for a world where people have time to repair a hole in a trouser. And where this, even in money terms, this makes sense.

Instead of buying a trouser for 5 euro's at the shop, but leaving a trail of misery in the world: it was probably produced in a 'sweat' shop in China, carried around the wold by polluting planes, boats or trucks. But that you do not see. Well, you know it now. The choice is yours.

I worked 10 years in the middle of the 'Beast' territory to learn (money system / banks). And I had to experience myself the evil these institutes bring to the world (I was jammed by a mortgage). So now I know how it feels. It feels like hell. I now see it as my path I had to go through, to be able to do the things I do nowadays.

I survived my suicide attempt. And now I feel happy that I am able to tell about it all. And I hope you, we all will learn from it. Make use of my experience. And that we together can create and implement an alternative system.

About banks 'efficiency'

I think there is no area in Business were efficiency lies lower than within banks. Money grows at the banks back, so they have enough. During the time I worked at banks at least seven out of 10 projects failed. And these where million-dollar projects. A project at least costs about half a million, and it goes easily up to above 100 million euro for corporate broad projects / programs.

Why did they fail?

They failed to too ambitious plans of managers, or share holders,. Incapable staff, or bad luck. And at least 15% of the staff walking around at the banks is external. Hired. Those people are not hired for one or two months, I know a lot of 'consultants' (huh, *consultants*?), working longer at banks than the payroll staff. They reside there for years and years (I did that too, why not? Nice work, lots of money). I got up to 200.000 euro's a year. In the Netherlands this is more than the countries president earned... And I am not a anomaly. Especially freelancers earn that much. I like freelancers, far more than I like consultancy firms, but I think the should not ask more than say 1,5 times an average payroll salary. Thus asking not more than say 50 euro's an hour.

And why is that external staff necessary? It is because the own organisation has become so inefficient, lazy and incapable that they need mercenary's to do the job. It has nothing to do with 'scarce' knowledge. It is like what happens to all big organisations without organisational renewal: they get more and more inefficient, more and more people end up in holes and corners in the organisations where they do more damage than bring added values. And actually only letting the whole organisation 'die' will help.

This inefficiency is a direct consequence of the primary construction factors within the Iconomy (endless payroll contracts, competition, profit making and an endless growing government). All participants have incentives to leave it like this or make it worse: the people working at the bank (don't leave the bank, bound by golden chains, they can take a mortgage and pay only 3,5% interest for instance), external staff creating their own jobs (by bringing no solutions which make them indispensable), etc.

Non Sens.

The hiring of external staff is to camouflage the bank's own incompetence and a abundance of money. The same goes for the insane offshoring programmes in which -parts of- the organisation are removed to countries as India, Pakistan, etc. I have been in coordination of these kind of projects. I have written articles about it. I have seen the total chaos where a little adjustment had to be routes via the bank's internal ICT organisation, than via an 'service level manager' to the 'local' partner (like IBM), than towards India, and than the ICT component had to be put in production in the operations center in Amsterdam.

Didn't work.

And managers reporting nice figures. Well, we did more ICT system changes, 'finished' more projects, wasted more money, but added value was more about negative than productive. But that was not reported... And now probably each big bank has replaced quite some core functions to other countries. They already or will soon finally have to admit that it was a bad decision. And they will discover that it will be far more difficult to get the operations back to their home place than it was to remove it...

I do not want to be an accessory anymore

Well as said earlier, I have been working for about ten years at banks. I do not want to work there anymore. And I think there will be few bank managers willing to hire me after the words I said on the banking system. Maybe one day I will work again within the bank sector, but than to migrate the function into institutes with as sound base.

But I think it will not come that far. Banks will start to collapse. Money as we know it will start to collapse. And this process probably will go on for maybe even 20 odd years. And each organisation still alive will deny that it should make a transition into a new system. Each remaining bank function will be lead by managers which finally got there chance to be the big man. And they will not give the power away easily. Even if it leads to the 'death' in a cruel bankrupting instead of a nice and painless dismantling and migration.

I decided I do not want to work at banks any more. Because I am really tired of the inefficient working manner. The hypocrisy that via one way you have to work very detailed and following all kinds of project management and quality standards, and via the other hand the management creates such a waste and makes such stupid decisions. And I don't want to be a mercenary any more of the stock market, share holders and ego-managers. A whore of the system. And indirectly as slave, because I felt it was not good, but I didn't leave. Was it the money? Was it I just didn't see alternatives to use my talents? Was it the 'carreersyndrome[10]'. Well I liked the complexity of the domain I was working in (ICT, Financial processes and products, etc.), And I liked the challenge to get a project done in the jungle we call bank. I just wasn't aware of how evil the money system is. Or didn't want to see it, because... what then? It was my profession... we are all so deluded.

Anyway, the main reason I don't want to work there anymore is that I now so deeply feel and understand that in fact the whole banking sector is evil. Lending money for interest and forced repayment is a bad thing. And that is where banks are based on nowadays, that is their core business.

I had a turbo learning curve, because I broke down myself. I had time to take distance and wonder, do research and think. And thus I think I am some years ahead of many people who worked there with me. I only hope they will see and feel it too soon. And that that they decide to leave that system. And that they find another place to earn their lively hood, because they too have families, mortgages and their meals to be paid for.

And especially now I see an alternative, I cannot work for banks anymore. I cannot say 'ich habe es nicht gewusst' (a famous quote of German officers saying they did not know about the holocaust). I know. I know... and now you know too.

---

10 Within the Iconomy people are forced to specialise and specialise... as a consequence of 'survival of fittest' via the comparing curriculum viteas. And thus we have more and more tunnel visioned people, not knowing anything about other disciplines. And when you want to change you have a problem, so go on for 40 years in the same direction till you reach retirement...

Some notes:

- I - too - see that it is not a good idea that everybody working in the banking industry leaves it right away, even if it was possible for them. It would be sensible, though, that conscious and capable people start with creating an alternative for the present (monopolistic) banking system. We should at least create an alternative, a fail over[11].
- Economist are right when they say that interest as a concept is required to keep the present economic system running. Intrinsic in our present economic model is interest. And we are not able to takes this ingredient out of it and not ruining the total thing. The same goes for concepts like 'GDP', 'property' (as we know it), 'state deficit', etc. The present implementation of economy cannot run without the previous mentioned concepts. It consists of it. And a bank cannot exist without the host on which it parasites. It is one entangled entity. But... the hope is that once we see that the present economical *implementation* (which I have labeled Iconomy), can be replaced by another economical model. Like upgrading the system. Like a software module version 1.0 and replace it with module version 2.0. We can do that... Iconomy is *not* the same as economy!!! Economy stands purely only for 'the way of dong the housekeeping'. It says nothing in the pure sense about needing debt, interest, GDP, etc. That is what we made it into in the past say 200 years. But we can leave that way of viewing. Once we take a look outside the box...

The final blast: leaving the Golden Standard / fractional reserve banking

Back to our tale: the creation of money and banks.

---

11 Term used in production systems as an alternative circuit or system to take over operations when the primary system halts or breaks down.

Figure: Zeitgeist Moving Forward Movie, making clear that fractional reserve banking will probably soon deteriorate the whole banking system [Time stamp: at 1 hour, 10 minutes]

The level of money creation had increased at a far higher pace than I have been talking about until now (which is already pretty insane). At a certain moment the 'economy' started to halter. It could not deliver the increasing demands in interest.
Banks couldn't lent new more money, even with the fractional reserve banking concept. New methods had to be found to create more money. It was then it was decided to leave the golden standard. Banks started to sell gold to get new money, or more important: they could create new money without the physical gold as counter value restriction.

Again a form of 'geotheft' (stealing from the total population) took place. The banks started to sell things (gold) which wasn't even theirs. So now, we ended up in a money system in which in fact the banknotes are not covered by gold. But, in that case, what covers the value of the note?

The answer: You paying tax.

The banks soundness is guaranteed now by the fact governments back them up. The recent bank buy outs are only 'little events' before the final blasting Tsunami. Because it is really the last resort. As the Zeitgeist movie states it: "Countries can bail out banks, but what if countries go bankrupt? Is there another planet that can bailout a whole planet?". And this is what is happening with Greece, and soon other countries...

It has gotten completely out of hand. We are approaching the ravine in a higher and higher speed. And politicians only talk about how to avoid 'a new crisis'. Deaf and dumb they must be. Open the eyes and realise the way we are on is completely wrong. But what goes for us personally goes for the system we choice: In the words of Led Zeppelin, Stairway to Heaven: "It is never to late to change the road you are on".

New concepts like a 'Ltd based on free floating stocks' are the latest phenomena in this age of insanity. Stocks leverage the money creation extremely. Example: a company releases it shares at the stock market. It sells 100.000 stocks. De stock market, or better: the people buying shares, like me and you, pay 10 dollar per share. The 'market value' of this company is suddenly 1 million dollar.

Via speculation, nice profit announcements (maybe even with some lies included) and a general economic trend upwards, the share price rises to 20 dollar each. Suddenly 1 million dollar has been created out of nothing. But what happens if I bought say 1000 stocks at 10 euro (for 10.000 dollar) and now sell them for 20.000 dollar (at stock price 20)? Could it be that directly the money in your pocket lowers in money, because the newly created 10.000 euro enter the free money circuit? Intrinsic inflation?

This example makes at least clear that the money market dynamics has become very -far too- complex. And modeling too long, or trying to grasp it into too much detail will make you end up in the mist. Were it wants you to be. Delusioned.

A personal note on stock trading

I myself have been doing transactions at the stock market for about 12 years. Intensively. I have had periods I 'traded' multiple transactions daily. At one moment I think I had about 300.000 euro's 'invested' in stocks and options. I created my own 'protection' fund by buying puts and so to defend my portfolio against strong movements down (via derivatives). I have dreamed for years that I could do good enough to make say 10 or 20% profit per year, and settle down at my early forties. Could stop working in the banking industry.

But than, at the end of 2007 my portfolio started to make big losses. Especially on banks. The bankruptcy of Fortis costed me about 70.000 euro's I guess, even with protection (otherwise losses would have been far bigger). I 2008 I decided to leave the market completely. I burned my fingers to deep. And I lost trust in the whole financial system. To my opinion it would only go down. It could take two or five years, but the fundamentals which I had gotten a clear insight into, and the dispositions in the banking economy where so bad, that to my vision it would be impossible to reach profit figures as we have seen in the nineties.

Buckets of mortgages from the Netherlands to the USA

I just (late 2007) had been part of a project within ABN AMRO to sell a bucket of mortgages[12]. Which didn't work out due to a worsening credit market. They had to be sold from ABN AMRO to General Electric. I got afraid of the whole housing market, I got afraid of my own mortgage, the price of our house and whether I would be able to keep on earning money as a consultant at banks (to earn the money I needed to pay my own mortgage). This combined with other things in my personal sphere got me jammed in my life.

[12] The idea behind such as deal is that the 'risk' of the mortgages weigh more on the balance sheet of a financial institution than of a non financial, due to banking legislation. So the risk on the mortgages (non repayment of the loan) is transfered to General Electric, and so is the profit. What the world does not know is that risks are not seen on the radar of the financial controllers at national banks anymore, and that these bombs now reside at company's allover the world. Once the housing market drops in the Netherlands, General Electric could explode due to it (if the deal had went on). Nice no?

A strange faith.

After my personal crash, I was lucky to sell our house at a price so that we didn't ended up with debt. A wonder for us. Two weeks after selling our house a next decline in Dutch house market set in...

I woke up out of a delusion. In a very hard way. I first had to experience hell (2008 was for me merely living in hell). Now I know and feel for example that when you buy a stock (share), with the intention to sell it tomorrow at a higher price, in fact your intention is to steal. To make money out of nothing. Economists and business man camouflaged this saintest fact. The connecting 'system' complex camouflages the facts. It scrambles all transactions in such manner so that we don't see anymore the ones who we steal from. And we even often don't realise that we are the ones who get stolen from. So stock trading I see nowadays as a immoral thing to do. Trespassing goodvalue no 2: do not steal (the intention to steal for me is almost as bad as doing it).....

Here too, I was not conscious. I didn't know. I didn't see, or did not want to see. Blinded too by what 'wise people' told me. And probably ignoring my feeling it was not right. But now I know, about the 'secret' of the present stock market. And you know it too. Feel free to spread this message. If you want a better world, and take action yourself: sell your stocks, and do something useful with the money. Even just leaving it on a bank account is better than to put them in stocks, in present stock market.

Stocks: Back to essence?
One final note: if the stock market did stay at its origination, in which it helped collect capital for joined ventures, there would not be a problem. There is nothing wrong with putting 'money' together in such way to create synergy to get a big thing going, which otherwise wouldn't have taken off. The ships of the VOC (Dutch sailing fleet in the middle ages) wouldn't have build if the concept of 'shares' wasn't introduced. In fact Dutch people have

had a big contribution in the creation of the stock market.

The problem is the profit making thing and free floating stocks. I will not elaborate in this here, watch the Zeitgeist movie on it, or read some good books on this topic.

I would see it as a big honor to undo the damage done from within the Netherlands, in the same way as 'we' contributed in the creation of the problem. Wall street is actually a Dutch name 'Waal straat' (the 'Waal' is a Dutch river). In the chapter on 'Primary Iconomy Constructors' I will talk about 'symmetric stocks' which make a step in a more sound direction. I hope to contribute in the engineering of new 'economic' concepts which have not the destructive elements in them which nowadays stocks, and especially all those derivatives and 'complex' financial instruments have.

For banks it is the same: if they had stuck to their essence, maintaining the currency flow, there would not be a problem. Now banks are camouflaged casino's: you bring there your money with the intention it takes care of it, and the next day you hear the bank 'invested' (gave it as a loan) to a company which has gone bankrupt, and thus the bank goes bankrupt and thus your money is gone. And the bank directors and shareholders are protected by 'business law' to share in the consequences. They go with a big bonus.

Gambling is wrong no? Or at least it was not the intention of our money to bring it in a deposit. The marble halls and nice shining buildings are just a facade of a gambling institute. People working at the bank might deny this. They cannot see through the delusion (yet). But they will, I hope, soon. We all will. That is the sign of the time, the Zeitgeist, we all open our eyes sooner or later, or go nuts.

Create a good bank?

I have spent many days on investigation and on my drawing board how to create a good-bank. A bank which does not create devastation, did not use the deposit to transform them into debt and mortgages. I even have written memo's to DNB (The Dutch National Bank). More and more I came to the conclusion it was not possible. At last, a freethinking woman, Fanny, gave me the final vision: "With some twinkles in the eyes, she said: but Iwanjka, why should the new bank be connected to DNB? Can't it be a system separate of the present money system?".

At first I started to create arguments why this wasn't possible or practical. Though I had been thinking in this direction already in some moments, but each time I was blocked in my thinkings because it went to far beyond comprehension.

But Fanny's words entered my conscious I guess and more and more I started thinking about it, leading towards to conception of a concept I called 'goodvalue trading' in spring 2009. At that moment I was residing at a friends (Bertus and Helouisa) place in Montpellier. The concept probably was planted in my dream or something, because it just was there when I woke up. Bertus has been going over the world for about 40 years visiting cacao farmers, that made me connect the 'bank concept' with the question how to create a system that people in the Netherlands could directly buy / trade with farmers allover the world: "One kg of cacao for a teddy bear we don't use here anymore?"

It was too simple to be true. I always had the vision that banks had to be big and complex. To opposite is true. You can read more on an possible currency alternative in the section on 'chivi' (the spoken form of GV, standing for 'GoodValue'), in the design chapter of the 'Flowconomy' eco subdomain.

"The body of a grown adult contains about five liters blood. When it gets more the heart will not be able to pump it around. When the veins get blocked the limbs will die or start malfunction"

The **banks (B usiness)** have put far too much blood in the body. The **gOvernment** have blocked the veins far too much (tax, regulations, bureaucracy). Both continue making it worse. The heart gets closer and closer to its infarct.

--- This is not the right road to course on ---

7 About the Hidden Loss Gap

I recently started to wonder how it is possible that efficiency of processes and operations in business and government easily rise for 5% each year, and that we only have to work harder and longer (retirement date) each year too. I state the hypothesis that efficiency rises for at least 5% each year on what I have seen myself working in the banking and government sector. Some examples about rising efficiency:

I Google on a certain thing I look for, and I find it within minutes. This would take in 'earlier times' days, or wasn't even possible. I send an email instead of writing a letter by hand (which would take days to arrive). I twitter about the things I do, and I encounter people doing the same, and we can share our energy and cause. Synergy, or at least synergy potential rises in a tremendous pace.

When I combine this with recent news headings in the Netherlands where politicians state that the retirement age should be increased, I only can come to the conclusion that somewhere the economy is leaking in a huge way.

Of course, economist say that the increased demand on labor is generated because of our higher living standards, our 'consumeritis', etc. I don't buy for that. I believe this will only result in a minor increase on labor, or not at all because we (can) do things so much more efficiently, for example by automation.

Than, when I look around in our society, I see so many processes which in fact do not add value at all, or are implemented in a clumsy manner, that it is a wonder this society is still running at all.

Take a look at the pumping around of tax money and giving it away as subsidies. Tens of thousands people government staff is fully occupied with this pumping around of money. And all those people sending in requests, and trying to keep the stream running. All that paperwork... adding no real value to our society (in my opinion). The same goes for the stock market, and financial system. Millions of highly payed staff is working in that business. Shuffling around 'financial products' and trading packages of debt: I cannot see any added value in it to our society. In the opposite: it deprives our society from its values, and it brings suffering and decay (at places the 'rich people' don't look, or prefer to close their eyes for, such as the poorest countries int this world).

Or all those silly tax rules and processes. For each little thing the government system creates a rule and a new process. In the Netherlands only running the tax engines costs 2 billion euro's a year. On about 17 million inhabitants, or say 10 million adults. Strange.

And I think the costs of all those 'services' gaining from this cancer work doubles at least this amount: the tax consultants, administration offices. More and more people are forced to hire specialised experts to do their yearly balance sheet work. It has become so complex, people cannot do it them selves anymore.

Entrepreneurs are more and more crushed under this load which they have to carry, but add in fact no value. And it only becomes more, because the people advising our government board are the same people who earn money with it via the consultancy firms, lawyer agencies, etc. Take a look at the curriculum vitae of the 'Raad van State' members, the highest political board in the Netherlands: you will only see (ex)-lawyers, former judges, etc.

I couldn't find a delegation of entrepreneurs, or 'ordinary people'.

An interesting thing is that you have to pay 'sales tax' when you buy or sell something. It is called 'added value' ('BTW' in Dutch). I more and more come to see this tax as 'decreased value'.

This concept for me has a high resonance with hidden loss gap. More and more a sort of cancer is consuming the life essence of its carrying host (the society).

And we are told that it is good that all those people are working in use less processes, it good for the economy, that it is good for us. Well, indeed, the Beast (Iconomy) grows upon it, but it is not good for our living habitat or for us. So this is a fallacy syndrome, see the appendix on Five Syndromes of Misery Creation.

So this is why we have to work harder and harder. And this is why each time where in the economy a certain relief emerges by automation or so, it is replaced by some useless process, just to keep the Iconomy running. And this the Beast grows.

I was happily surprised when I watched the Zeitgeist Moving Forward movie, and saw this diagram:

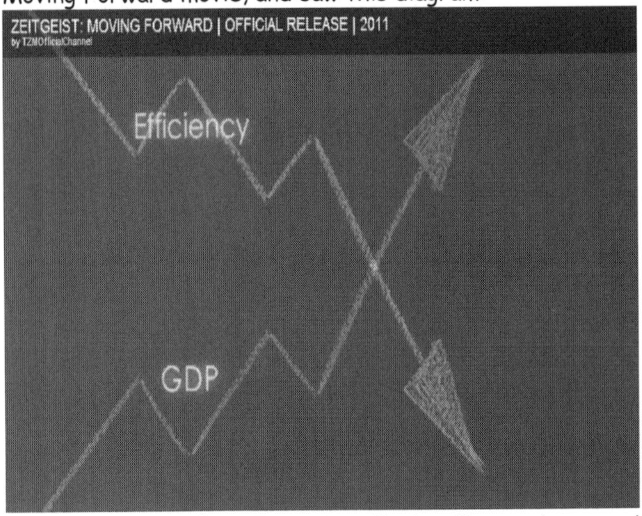

Figure: Screen shot Zeitgeist Moving Forward, around minute 52 - The higher the GDP the lower the efficiency.

In fact the movie says the same: where economist say things are going 'better' and economics 'indicators' show 'improvement', in fact the level of efficiency drops. And the only reason that we can 'consume' that inefficiency is by improvements of automation, and technology. This camouflages the huge in-efficiency in present system, which - I think - easily outweighs the 'inefficiency' of the notorious USSR systems.

The GDP rate is highly correlated to...taxes and 'moving things around'. Because each movement causes new tax to be paid. And the things 'moving around' are becoming more and more sense less: the further you drive for your work: more GDP, the more fuel your car consumes: more

GDP, the more people getting sick and needing 'care staff': the more GDP, more people working for the government: more GDP...

That is why we should create a common services eco function (the equivalent of government), which is not 'fed' by (a ratio) of the GDP... because that will always lead the sooner or later to a 'economic efficient' but social-lowvalue system. A matter of time and system dynamics, system evolution.

And in fact, one of the deeper reasons the government system keeps growing is because everybody needs money nowadays. Where in early days, everybody or every little community is self providing, now practically nobody is anymore. And we all need money. So, even if somebody working at the government finds he or she is doing something useless, they cannot leave, simply because they have to pay their rent, or the interest on their mortgage - which is a sort of rent as well[13] - too.

> "As long as we are tied to the present money system we will be bound to the Iconomy. (and a crashing money system[14])"

It is interesting to mention that the Venus Project draws

[13] In Dutch the word 'interest' is 'rente'. Sounds like 'rent', no? And in fact: the principle is the same: you have to pay money to somebody else, based on the fact that the other possesses what you use.

[14] I mention this, because also from country sake perspective governments should -directly- decide to introduce a local currency next to the euro. There should be an alternative, a fail over. As a safety measure, Greece should do this. But the Netherlands too. A simple deduction on country risk management... and if we do create a new currency, learn from the past and make it a chivi type (no intrinsic inflation and no debt). And see which money system evolves best...

a vision of a real 'efficient' world. In this world we can work far less hours and have the same or even a better life standard. This is achieved by doing our 'economy' in a *real* economical way. See the chapter on Flowconomy too for practical proposals on this. It has highly to do with eliminating the causes of the hidden loss gap. And with eliminating the 'Primary Iconomy Constructors', see the chapter with this title.

The Venus Project goes a step further and even eliminates money completely. And in which machines and ICT do the work. In which machines build our houses. I personally long more for a world in which we find time and pleasure to build our own houses with recycled wood. But in both visions the kernel is the same: eliminate useless competition. Eliminate inflation-money. Eliminate economy-driven waste and 'consumeritus'. And do things in a global way. Sharing global resources. Use technology in a smart way, and use the *possibilities* for creating new social organizing models.

8 Democratic Dictatorship?

Next to the money system our 'people organisation' is crucial for our habitat. Some words on the 'democracy' we are living in. Democracy literally means something like 'the power' (cracy) to the people (demos).

Well we at least can vote each four year...

Democracy literally means something like 'the power' (cracy) to the people (demos).

Well we at least can vote each four year...

But... what in fact is my influence? I think I sent 50 pretty good ideas into this 'democratic' system with the hope the 'leaders' would pick them up, or at least look at them and give me a reasonable answer why the ideas should *not* be implemented.

Nothing I heard. I send message to political parties. Even to Wouter Bos (a previous minister of the Finance department).

Why?

Because the channels towards the 'brains' of our organism are completely congested. The brain seems only occupied with who is the boss in the brain, without taking notice of the other parts of the body.

And who are the ones who decide the course of this country? It is the lobby-ist of multinationals influencing politicians. Those people who are the survivalists of the fittest competition. The ones who can scream the loudest, or can play the dirty game called politics in the 'best' way.

Well, I don't buy that.

I don't what those people to be my leaders.

So, the system which should makes sure that this wouldn't happen does not work?

Yes, it is corrupt. Broken.

I call this 'corrupt' political system an 'Egocracy'.

My hypothesis is, that we do not live in a true democracy. In fact live in a dictatorship. The dictator which I see is representing at max 1 percent of the population and services especially the present system, the iconomy, the richest and 'powerful' (the ceo's, (ex) executives, the career-politicians[15], old boy friends network, monarchy, etc).

And the ordinary people are deluded with a system which has been almost illegally called 'democracy'. And the whole system is orchestrated in such way that it services maximally the Iconomy and the previous mentioned 1% of the population.

Logically.

And the political party system is maybe the best example. Divide and conquer. Ceasar already did do that. Parties fighting in the arena instead of working together. Is this Utopia? No.

How much longer are we going to buy this?

Well, the system is rapidly decaying, that is the good news.

You may vote, but your vote gets not heard. My conclusion.

In the Netherlands since the coming of the Internet, applications called 'stemwijzers' (freely translated: voting

[15] People who have as occupation 'being politician' and being it for years and years, and probably never worked in other areas, or lost connection with it...

helpers) are very popular. I guess most people who have voting right, first go to such an application, fill in about 40 questions, get their party advice, and than go voting.

Isn't it already a sign at the wall that people need those applications to chooce? And often the party which is primary suggested really does not make sense in the eyes of the one asking for advice.

Than I thought, why is it that the input of those applications is not used by some kind of national steering team? To take in consideration the peoples will, make a plan how to put it to practice in a harmonic and practical manner? The Harmonicracy was born...

"Than I thought, why is it that the input of those applications is not used by some kind of national steering team to take in consideration the peoples will, make a plan how to put it to practice in a harmonic and practical manner? The ***Harmonicracy*** *was born..."*

Why should my 'expression' on what I want first be aggregated into a party direction, and than that party I vote for hopefully gets elected, than it has to make compromise with other parties, and than you think something is left from the original voters desire or **voting expression**? I don't think so.

We are blinded sheep. High time to stop this puppet-show.

And than I do not talk about the sense striking Idiotery of ego based parties, which will not listen to good ideas of other parties because they might loose voters when they cooperate publicly with another party. A synergy killing mechanism. Populism. Stupidness. I cannot think of other words, than these to qualify our present political system, especially compared to possible alternatives I see glooming (more on this at the Harmonicracy chapter, in the redesign part of this book).

And of course, the system we have now is far better than the monarchy which may countries experienced in the middle ages. But time chances, and way not choose for a next, far better alternative? Especially, when taking in consideration, that the present political system is even not *able* to fulfill the requirements we have nowadays on our organizing system.

The present system is *not able* to give the response on the questions the Zeitgeist of this moment raises. Watch the movie and you'll know. Or even worse: the present political system is a crucial part of the problem, and the reason why our economy and ecology is breaking down.

About the role of classical mass media television

And I joined a television show called 'Rondom10'. The idea we could say something, I raised my arm for about 15 minutes, but was kept keenly out of the picture by the camera crew. Only the -pre orchestrated[16]- 'debate' of the guests in the middle of the audience got the microphone. And who are the ones asked for such debates? People who join the game. Tell the same stories, radicalise and provide for a high amount of watchers.

---

16 By 'chance' my ear catched an conversation between a producer of the program and a panel member : "Producer, yeah, you did good, things went such as we reviewed at forehand, no?". The panel member was really excited on being on television, seemed he would say anything to be on television... strange world.

Since I experienced this whole thing more than ever I believe everybody should kick his or her television out of the house immediately. You *think* you watch an open debate, but it is *all* orchestrated. And program makers create maximum friction. They do not desire a better society.. they are part on of the egocracy and Iconomy. And as long as people want this, they will get the society according to it... so high time to make up our minds...

I would plead to not anymore do political things on television... no hyped debates anymore. Let politicians do their work via one on one in the fields, write a book or so, have a good program. And we have the social media now, no? Let people decide for themselves based on reason, not on propaganda and commercial biases of the media industry.

My experiences in politics - New Netherland

Some last notes: I was part of the creation of a new political party in the Netherlands, called 'New Netherland', as a campaign leader I was confronted with the fact that all kinds of 'voting assistance tools' neglected the new parties. So even if our program was more reasonable, the voter would not be forwarded to our party, because we were blocked from entering the game! And as I write this, regional elections are taking place. A new coming party, called 'Party of the Animals[17]', was blocked from taking part in a national television debate. Only the 'establishment' was allowed to join. So, guess

[17] Who would have thought a party with this name would make it to the chamber, but it did. Probably because is has a face. People are so sick of mainstream parties, that a party standing for something inspired a lot of people to vote on it, even if it is a single issue party (animal and nature sake). It is interesting to see that people tend to 'topic oriented' parties (spiritual, animals, elderly, etc.), and not 'left, middle, right'. This observation has been an important marker for the design of the Harmonicracy eco subdomain.

which parties are getting the votes? Yes, the say five parties which do not wanna change anything, doing a sort of muppet show debate one television, on minor issues.

So, no matter what party the votes choses for within the group in this debate, nothing is gonna change.

And that is exact who the Iconomy likes it. No change.

"Give the people bread ant plays"
[Dutch: "Geef het volk Brood en Spelen"]

> *The dictator has no worries as long as he keeps the people animated (Plays in the Arena) and dumb. But what if the people awake?*

9 Primary Iconomy Constructors (PIC)

Before redesigning a new system, we should analyze which factors are responsible for the negative side and trend of our economy. Once we have these elements, we can design a new system and state as a requirement that at least these factors should not be present. I wanted to identify the three most dominant factors. After three years elaboration, I come to:

1. **Accountability avoidance and profit making**. We talk a lot about responsibility, but when it comes to taking a consequence from entrepreneurship our leaders in business have still a lot to learn... Profit making stands for the senseless ways companies (and western countries) plunder the world. The zeitgeist movement also sees profit making as one the the roots of the evil.

2. **Debt & money creation**. I have talking a lot already on this topic in the 'Money' chapter...
3. **The GDP Beast**. I talked already about the BOMb complex (Business gOvernment, huMan). The gOverment grows on GDP creation, as the banking sectors grows on money and debt creation.

In the part of this book about redesign you can read about an alternative economic implementation, named F*lowconomy*, in which the previous factors have been removed... it can be done.

9.1 PIC I – Accountability & Profit Making

Something I which I learned in my 10 years banking experience, is that the thing 'profit making' is a phenomenon, which creates a highly destructive element in our economy.
Maybe saying 'Profit Taking', is a better expression: mostly a thing is litery taking something from others, or the environment, not being in balance.

About juridical entities
Sorry, most of you probably do not like juridical matters and so. But to understand the evil of this constructor, you'll have to absorb some information on juridical entities (the things business is done in). The good news: within the Flowconomy these concepts are abandoned, so the world will get a lot more simple!

A thing I only came to see in the last few years is that the 'juridical entity' in which 'business' is encapsulated is actually pretty strange. Every entrepreneur which leaves its employer-employee contract and heads for the world of the free market sees himself confronted with the question: "What do I have to do legally and fiscally to get my company going?".

You consult the Wikipedia on the possible formats, you consult the tax office and Internet. Soon, this quest leads you to the 'advice' of an accountant. The law demands that your financial housekeeping gets a yearly approval by an accountant, so there you go.

The accountant quickly makes clear that there are several possible vehicles to wrap your company in, regarding from a foundation format towards limits (Ltd's), and some mixed formats in between. "Don't do the foundation format, because than you are personally accountable in case of a claim", the accountant says, at least this is the case in the Netherlands.

And: "If you want to be able to capitalise your business you should at least take a format like a Ltd, because than you can issue stocks".

And so I did myself. Somewhere at the beginning of 2003 I established two Ltd's, to be able to work as a free person. One Ltd was called 'IT-Inspiration', and was established to act as 'operational vehicle', and to catch claims, if my customers would sue me, and the other one was called 'Holding Inspiration' which was created to aggregate wealth. This was the 'treasure' Ltd. The Holding would send a bill periodically to the working vehicle to transfer money. The working vehicle should stay as cashless as possible. The working vehicle sends bills to customers (in my case banks), for the hours worked as consultant.

And, the 'director' of IT-Inspiration is not 'Iwanjka', no it is 'Holding Inspiration Ltd'. So an additional defense line was build to catch the possible torpedo's from customers to my private person. A two hurdle barrier.

Why am I telling all this?

I tell this because 'big businesses' are organised in the same way. And far more complex. The 'business men' take cover behind mass of defense lines. They can create all kinds of bad things, take huge risks, and can get away with the profits. Losses are for the ones who gave credit, but more in general: for society as a whole. This we have seen with the numerous bank bailouts, the same we see with countries like Greece: bankers and big companies made a mess by lending money to Greece in the first place, and now the whole society has to pay because Greece may not collapse. And who profits? Yes, correct: banks, and the parties holding the shares of the banks. Did you know the FED (the American Central bank) is not property of the state? So the bigger the debt of the state, the bigger the gains of certain parties... not a good incentive for a organisation that should bring a stable money market...

Well, it even gets even worse: the economic system dynamics invented another construction to keep the real stakeholders out of the wind: The shareholders, holding the stocks of the Ltd. They are completely not accountable for the actions done on their behave. They are actually the ones giving steerage to the company via shareholder meetings. They are the superiors of the CEO's.

But the Iconomy structures made things so complex,

created so much mist, that accountability and responsibility in the business domain is completely gone. The accountability is dispersed over tens of thousands of stockholders. Even you and I probably are actually accountable, because we 'own' stocks via whatever way. Via direct 'investments' in our personal funds, or via retirement funds, whatever.

Hedge funds, collapsing banks, escaping CEO's, etc.

The consequences of this 'accountability-avoidance syndrome' we have seen and experienced. It made Enron collapse. It made Icesave collapse. It made Iceland go bankrupt. It made a country as the Netherlands double its national debt in about five years, and in fact made it virtually bankrupt already too (even though our leaders mention nothing about this, they mention nothing about hundreds of billions in liabilities at banks balance sheets, directly hitting its inhabitants when eg. house prices drop). Or maybe they don't know. Our leaders are often not that wise as we esteem them...

The previous CEO of ABN AMRO, Rijkman Groenink, the failing bank got 20 million euro's when he left, the Dutch people paid 20 *billion* euro's for his 'work'. Off course this is not the work of Rijkman alone, it is the combined expression of all involved people. Tens of thousands of employees of the bank, tens of thousands of stock holders, the Dutch banking authorities, etc. Rijkman was only the concentration point of all this madness and stupid steering.

But what I want to make clear is that *all* Dutch people did bleed, and 99% of those people where *not* the ones who were the gamblers. *They* did *not* work at the bank, do *not* get huge salaries and nice mortgage arrangements. They did *not* get year in year out huge profit payout for the stocks. They are the ordinary civilians, paying taxes and working for low wages...

That is why I want to make clear. The risk-profit balance for people who are related to the bank, and who are not, are completely out of hand. It would be fair that the people taking the risk pay for the 20 billion. Now they don't and get even a huge bonuses, and keep there job, more safe than ever because the bank has now become a government department, funded by tax payers.

This is a *direct* consequence of the accountability avoidance mechanism of Ltd's and free floating stocks, or say 'current stock implementation'.

That is way I propose to make a change, that new entrepreneurs choose a foundation as vehicle. And that our society -via taxes- balances the profit-risk balance: Ltd's pay for all the costs they created for society, and they pay for a risk premium (chance that things go deeply wrong, like what is happening now in the world).

Ideally, the Ltd format would be banned immediately, but this is not feasible at this moment. Therefore I propose a migration path, which may take say 20 years to migrate the most of the businesses into sound, sense making formats. Or better: entrepreneurs may choose: do it as a Ltd, but be completely accountable for losses as well, including their shareholders.

And, each individual has the power for change: just select only vendors or services organisations with a foundation as its underlying format when you buy goods or services. Change will come automatically. You can change this world. Novaglobe intends to start publishing per product line or field of services, which organisations fulfill flowconomy guidelines. Via this way 'ladders' are created, the goodest stand at the top.

> ***Iconomy Constructor I***
> *"People an organisations avoid accountability for their behaviour via constructions like the Limited (Ltd). In times of profits the shareholders, directors and employers gain. In times of losses, the society pays. Profit-Loss is not balanced over the responsible people and society."*

Symmetric Stocks?

A last thing on stocks. It would help also tremendously when we would replace present 'asymmetric stocks' (with non balanced risk-profit proportions for shareholders and the rest of the society), towards symmetric stocks.

We could create a 'SymmetricLtd' as a juridical format, and we could say that new stocks may only be issues as symmetric stocks. In this case stockholders are in the same way accountable for lingering debts if the company goes bankrupt, as they are for profits when the company flourishes.

Huh, debt?

And why is it actually that there can be a problem when a company collapses?

One word is enough: debt.

Or stated in a more general way: taking liabilities which are not covered. And that is what banks do nowadays.

So, now we bump into the second Iconomy Constructor: Debt.

9.2 PIC II - Debt & Money Creation

In the Netherlands I call the mortgage stimulation system 'NederlandsLeed', the international term I use is 'DutchDouleur'. There is no country on this world with so relative high house prices and debt per person. Economist say that is because our country is so small. Nonsense. The Beast at work, direct consequence of Iconomical system dynamics at work.

What goes up, will come down. Sooner and sooner now. Our Pride will lead us into misery. People in the Netherlands blame for instance the USA people for being so stupid and reckless to have so much debt. In the Netherlands we have more. We are deluded... And we blame the people in Greece for being so stupid that the land got into this worse condition. Well, wait and see what happens in the Netherlands once the 'dykes break' (housing prices).

And in opposite to the people in the USA, in the Netherlands we cannot give the key together with the debt back to the banks. We loose the house and keep the dept. So smart we are in the Netherlands... Hobbits we are.

And people are starting to notice, or at least, their emotion is. Leading them to vote on (extreme) materialistic and non-social political parties (VVD -PVV-CDA) combination. Interesting to note is that all of these parties are led by striving egoistic-feeling men. As long this fear for the housing market is not eased, people will not vote on other parties, even when the VVD-PVV complex leads us into a (Islam-fear) driven war....

> "In the Netherlands big misery is at hand due tax-interest-reduction stimulated high housing process. I call this 'DutchDouleur', in Dutch I named it 'NederlandsLeed'.

About lending in general:
Again, I don't get it anymore. As a child I was told I first had to gain enough money to be able to buy an ice cream. This could take easily two weeks, saving pennies, before I was able to buy this highly desired object.

Once I am an adult people start to tell me that I really, really should take a loan of easily about 300.000 euro's to buy a house. "If you do not do that, you are a thief of your own wallet!". "No, no, no, this is different than the ice cream you once had so save money for".

Bull shit.
A Fallacy Syndrome (see appendix) of the highest category. BO-complex at work. Once the house prices start to drop the BOMb is gonna burst.

The only reason why we are put into this illusion is because it is the only way banks can continue making there huge profits, and government can sell our own lands to us at tremendous prices: in the Netherlands the selling of land is one of the most important income factors to pay the salaries of government staff with....

More in general, banks *need* debt. Without putting us to debt, banks would go bankrupt directly.

Figure: Zeitgeist Moving Forward movie, making clear that our current money system is entwined with the debt balloon. Time stamp in the movie: 1 hour, 11 minutes. Only by replacing the money system as we know it completely, we can get rid of the debt balloon...

Money is debt. And debt is stealing, as this Zeitgeist scene makes clear:

Figure: Zeitgeist moving forward, time stamp 1 hour, 22 minutes.

And... that nice and shiny new house fits in our own weak spot: our own greediness and materialism. We forgot that we also could live in a hut (or camper) in the forest. As from our early days our collective dream is to have our own house. A little bit bigger than our friends houses.

And, in a intriguing way, our government does not arrange for houses which are affordable and suited for families to live in. Neither does it allow us to build them ourselves (yes, If can pay tons of euro's you may. Maybe).

Together with nice tax reductions (a strange pact with the banking industry), people are pulled into buying houses, or better: getting themselves married to banks and debt. People think *they* have the house, in fact *the bank* has the house and *you* have the *debt*... Nowadays

60% of the households in the Netherlands are bound by debt for their houses and have a mortgages for on averages somewhere between 100.000 and 300.000 euro's. So they are sitting on a time bomb, ready to explode. Once the housing prices drop, like it happened in the USA, the bombs explode. Leaving a trail of devastation. Mortgages are financial nuclear bombs. And financial derivatives. And Warren Buffet was right when he said that financial derivatives are weapons of mass destruction. When talk about banning machine guns (after the gunman disaster in Norway), but nobody sees the far more deadly weapons in our midst: mortgages. They are allowed, and promoted by the governments... Google on 'suicide' and 'mortgage', count the hits, and you know.

60% of the households in the Netherlands have a mortgage. They are sitting on a time bomb.

They *live* in a time bomb.

People think: "Even if I loose my job, and cannot pay for the rent of the mortgage, we can sell the house". Wrong. When things go down in the economy, house prices will drop sharply, and they will find themselves caught in a situation they cannot escape from: they cannot sell the house, because the selling price is not enough to pay off the mortgage. And they cannot pay the interest anymore. They will find themselves like as in an elevator with broken cables, going down, and they cannot escape...

A little observation on which I will come back in the Togetherhood section: I believe that the most 'harmonic' (senseful) living habitats are not habitats with one or two adults and one, two or three children. I believe that habitats where say up to seven children and up to say 14 adults can share a house hold (with their own private rooms) is far more harmonic. But... this the banks do not like, who should be the contractor for the mortgage contract? And the Iconomy does not like so many people living together, taking care for the elderly amongst them themselves, of sharing the care of the children. Or the sick. That will cost GDP (PIC3) and Profit (PIC1).

No... people should work! Make money. Put the children in a crèche. The elderly in a old people house. The 'mentally sick' in a psychiatric institution. That makes money roll..

So, here we say several phenomena coming together. How the profit incentive, and the loan incentive and the GDP growth incentive hit directly into our most personal sphere: our living habitat.

> "The Iconomy wants people to be divided maximally, at a minimal amount of square feet"... [Iwanjka]

And, now countries are bailing out banks. And continental monetary entities (IMF, FED, EU bank), are bailing out complete countries like Greece and Iceland. But who is gonna bail out a whole planet (as the Zeitgeist movie says)?

Figure: Zeitgeist moving forward movie, time stamp: 1 hour, 18 minutes.

9.3 PIC III – The GDP Beast

PIC3: The GDP Beast

The nasty thing on discussion and elaborations on the present economical implementation, is that it leaves government often out. But the government is a highly influential factor. It is the one making deals with the 'Business' side. It is the one making rules and laws benefiting the profit machine, the banks, and companies.

And it is one of the biggest feeds for the Business. The government is giving the Business a lot of business and pays a lot of money for it. And both are happy to grow on and on. That is the nature of the beast. That is why I decided to include the government in the problem description, labeled with 'Iconomy'.

A man I highly value is Raoul Schepers. Like Ervin Laszlo he is one of the few -but numbers rise rapidly- who really understand the system dynamics. Who can see through the mist of delusion. And who worked himself years and years in the financial business (like I did too).

He did an analysis on why things felt to go deeply wrong, and why classical economists don't take notice of this. He discovered that the used economical models have some huge flaws in them. Keynes, Friedman, etc. Like Freud did in psychiatry, these man did in economy: they wanted so badly to state that they where the ones having *the* models, the truth (Me-Benefit Syndrome, see Appendix), that they just *created* models which covered the dynamics between a certain range in time ('symptoms') and claimed that they where holistic. They where wrong. They only modeled the external behaviour (what you see) about the system. Not how it works.

And they where in deed very intelligent. But their biggest talent probably was to be able to convince the world that they had the true models. Friedman convinced Thatcher. Thatcher convinced Reagan (see Zeitgeist Moving Forward movie).

And the 'only proper medicine' was put into action: sell more and more of the government goods. Privatise them. Nice money for the government. Sell energy companies, care, infrastructure. Free market, yeahh[18]! I even heard stories about Greece selling whole Islands. So the government start to sell things they a moralistic not allowed too. The island belong to the huMans, not a thing called 'Government'.

In fact the government, sold things they were not allowed to sell. They sold things which belonged to the community. Like the earth. And now the same community who already pays

---

18 Again: a free market is good. But only when the PIC's are taken out. See the Flowconomy chapter for a proposal.

high taxes to keep the government running, has to pay high prices for train tickets, care, etc. So they pay double. And the banks and companies are the happy ones. 'Making' (taking?) more money as profit.

GDP Beast

The essence of what Raoul discovered, and what I did not have clear yet, was that GDP-growth-desire is in everything. I already had defined the Fattening Syndrome[19], as a underlying principle for organisations in nowadays Iconomy in general.

But what he makes very clear in his presentations, and models, is that the government desires for a growing GDP. A higher GDP means that the government can hire more staff. Meaning that managers in the government are more satisfied in their growth desire (power, ego). And... that politicians can increase the budgets for their megalomaniac plans. As this budgets are percentages directly related to the GDP. And... if the GDP grows, the budget deficit (difference between the government income and expenses) may grow as well. And the government deficit (difference between income and expenses) is often stated as an percentage of the GDP, the deficit may grow as the GDP rises... get the picture?

Than, once realizing this, things become very clear from this perspective: why medical care is not preventive, but merely only reactive. The more people get sick, the more doctors have work, and have an income. The sum of incomes makes the GDP, so the GDP rises. The government is not happy when the medical care sector has less clients! So, nothing is *really* focused on prevention or a real structural cure. Or where it is stated, if quickly gets sabotaged. The same for examples children crèches, see the analysis chapter of the Togetherhood chapter: the separation of mothers and their children raises GDP! Another example: the more miles we drive for our work, the more petrol we need and cars break

[19] See Appendix 'Five Syndromes of Misery Creation'

down, the more GDP is being created... The GDP Beast does not want an efficient economy, because that would lower GDP...

Understand it?

As long as GDP is the food and the incentive of the government, things will hardly change. So, this is a requirement for the new design, for Novaglobe, to at least neutralise the GDP Beast.

9.4 Summary Primary Iconomy Constructors

This chapter is the kernel of this book. As soon as you grasp the Primary Iconomy Constructors, you are equipped to make sense full decisions on where to put your vote. As long as these constructors are present in our ecology, nothing will happen. No matter which party you vote on. And almost non of the established parties in your country probably intends to do a thing about it.

At this moment. The conscious for need the need of fundamental change is rapidly growing. More and more people see that politics lost control over our economy...

Probably because they just didn't knew. So tell them about it.

Or maybe the message was too big for the leading politicians to speak about. Afraid to speak this truth.

Every new creation will be structured based on the blueprint of the underlying constructors. We need to change the constructors. Only then we can build new houses. With fabulous shapes and atmosphere.

So the elimination of these *constructors* of the Iconomy are the *requirements* of the 'grand design'... for instance in the Flowconomy these constructors will be neutralised...

As a resume:

1. No more possibility of responsibility **avoidance** for those wanting to make profit. And, the concentration, the focus on possession needs to be dematerialised. For example the concept of the 'Ltd' as a organisation format is no good.
2. No more **debt** as we know it and (non-proportional) **money creation**.
3. No more governments which have a main incentive on **GDP growth**.

10 Part II – Design

Design concepts
In this chapter I shortly want to describe some important, for me inspiring, concepts.

10.1 About the global scale and Spiral Dynamics

A well known 'grow' model is Spiral Dynamics. Spiral Dynamics is a theory of human development introduced in the 1996 book Spiral Dynamics by Don Beck and Chris Cowan. It was used in the transition of the Apartheid in South Africa.

De whole chain is depicted below:

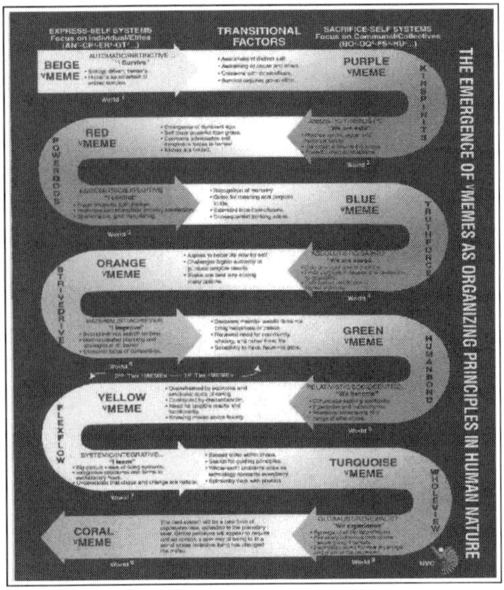

Figure: Spiral Dynamics stages.

For more information see eg. the Wikipedia.

What is really interesting is that this model sees a global organisation as the 'highest' level of growth and harmony (as far as defined in this model). The design of NovaGlobe fits seamlessly well in this viewpoint... See picture below, which is a capture of one of the latest stages:

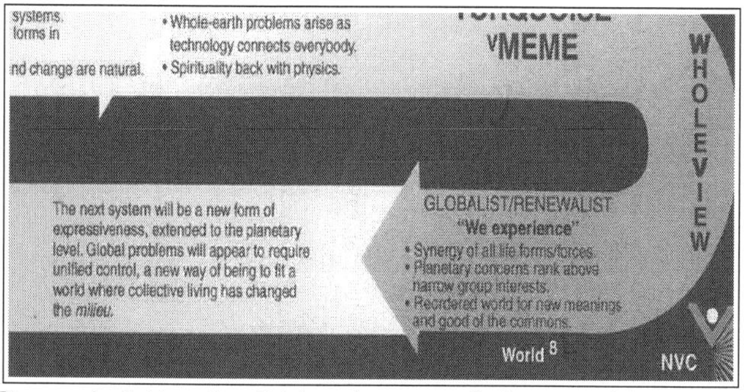

Figure depicting the 'highest' stage of the Spiral Dynamics: Create a global model.

This reinforces the idea and requirement to take a holistic / global scale for designing a new system...

10.2 The Flipped Maslow Pyramid...

I once read a book, which was also about creating a new world. It took the Maslow 'motivation model' as a basis. For those who do not know the model: its essence is fairly simple.

It states that first the most basic needs must be fulfilled for people or in society before other levels make sense. In other words: in does not make sense to try to talk about all kinds of collaboration systems between people as long as they starve due to a lack of food.

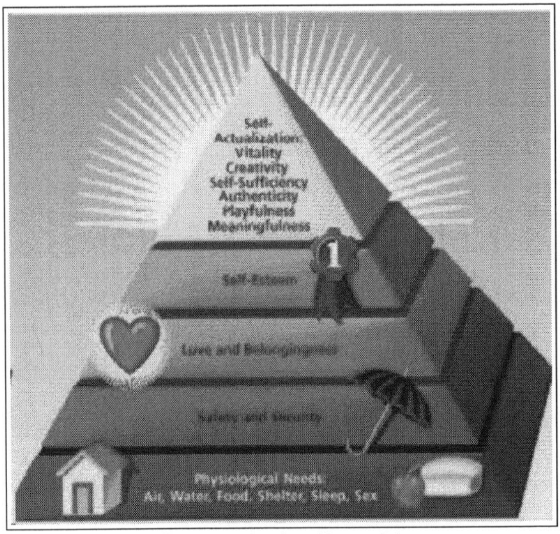

Figure: Maslow Pyramid.

But than, I thought: "Why is it, that we in the western countries have our bellies filled (and more than that), and still make wars, and each 1 out of 10 adults takes anti depressants? What goes wrong?". And in addition, a discussion was going on in the political party we set up on the topic of a 'base income for all. I learned that even Martin Luther King, already saw a base, unconditional income for all as a minimal foundation for a humane society.

I thought: "Well, we have a good social security in the Netherlands: when you loose your job, you get about 1000 euros a month from our social care system". But what I saw, was that for about 60% of the house holds, this was not enough. Why not? Because they took a debt to buy a house (mortgage). And in the Netherlands you get about 50% tax discount on your income tax, for the interest you pay to the bank. But once you loose your job, you loose not only your income, you loose also de ability to get interest back from the government. And it is quite usual people pay for about 800 euros mortgage interest to the bank. This costs them with a salary of say 3000 euro gross about 400 euro's net. But when the loose their job, they have to pay the full 800 euros each month. And that combined with the fact that their income drops from say 2000 Euro to 1000 Euro (social care).

That is crazy, no?

So, I thought: we can create a base income thing (meaning everybody gets about 1000 euro, and people can earn money on top of that), but than, the first thing people will do is buy more expensive houses and take a higher debt. The newly introduced money, which was intended to *free* people form there jobs in which they would otherwise be stuck, flows directly - of course - into the pockets of the banks, and people are even more stuck than in the situation without the base income.

I than got the picture of the Maslow pyramid, and thought "Hey, actually we have not moved into the top of the pyramid, we passed the top and entered a sort of reversed Maslow Pyramid". In this pyramid a sort of same situation resulted in the basis, as in the situation we did not even have enough food for our children to feed them. We again have not the 'mental' and practical space around us to do sense full things. We feel afraid of dropping house market. We feel afraid of loosing our jobs. Not because of that we wont get no money, it is because we put our selves far too deep in financial obligations. In bank balance terms: we have to much *liabilities*.

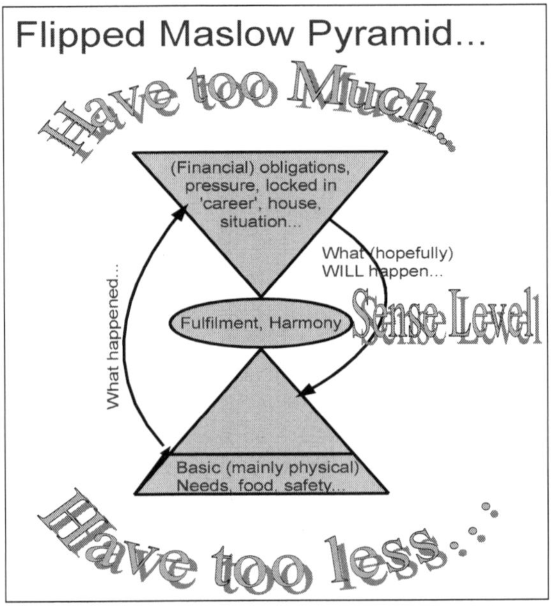

Figure: Flipped Maslow pyramid model: we now have food (Western countries) but a deprived from freedom, feel pressed, feel no sense in life, etc.

So, we arrived in our society in a similar situation as when we first had to arrange for food for all. And safety. And trust. But now caused by financial poorness, our own greed. And an insane -but logical- government-capitalistic dynamics.

We did a great job.

This also leads to a requirement for the construction of the new world: no more lending.

To put it in other words: all we do to help our 'economy' will not work, as long as we don not transform towards a non-lending society.

"There must be some kind of way out of here,"
Said the joker to the thief,
"There's too much confusion,
I can't get no relief.
Businessman they drink my wine,
Plowman dig my earth
None of them along the line what any of it is worth"

[All Along the Watchtower / Bob Dylan]

10.3 Examples of existing concepts

Much is already invented..

10.3.1 Zeitgeist movement and RBE

> The **Zeitgeist movement** is a global operating, conscious making movement, initiated by the film producer Peter Joseph. RBE stands for **Resource Based Economy**: an economic implementation without money, and with sense full sharing of resources globally.

I think it was about somewhere mid 2009 I saw fragments of the Zeitgeist movie for the first time. Interesting that a girl from Greece (a country now in deep financial turmoil) lead me towards it. For me it was a visual representation of many things I had discovered myself. Especially regarding the monetary system, the movie makes comprehensible for every one why it is not working (anymore) and why it is breaking down. It is not sustainable. And it also makes very clear we need a paradigm switch.

The only thing I did not like was that I felt a certain bias on conspiracy theories (to much the word 'they' was used I feel). For me, I believe in a combined working of destructive individual people combined with destructive systems. The composite behaviour of this system feels like some kind of intelligence is behind it. I think this is true, it is the combined intelligence of the destructive people and system. But I do not believe in world spanning conspiracies or (negative) new world orders. And even if they did exist: I do not want to fight them, I cannot win that battle, because violence and war is their territory, not mine. Bringing in enough light, transparency and good people will make them fade by itself. That is what I believe.

Back to Zeitgeist. So the movie I find ideal as an survey on becoming cognitive conscious. To understand the world we are living.

But... the movie I saw (Zeitgeist part II) it did not talk about a solution. I think that was also not the goal of the producer Peter Joseph.

Early 2011 I was invited for the press release of a new edition, 'Zeitgeist Moving Forward'. I must say: my conspiracy feeling was gone, and there was a substantial part dedicated to a concept called 'Resource Based Economy'. In this model global resources are divided in a reasonable manner. Production is not based on competition, and thus product become far more sustainable. Things are more and more produced in 'ecobalance' with the earth. And very important: the role of money has gone.

I think that eliminating money totally in a next increment of the economy implementation is a bridge to far, but the RBE gives a good view on how can do it differently. And It can be done... if we wish. And each of us starts to work for this.. 'be the change'...

10.3.2 The Venus Project

Practically directly after, I saw a glimpse of the Venus Project. The good thing about this movie / clip, was that it was about a holistic solution for tproblems today. Visions of a new world. I learned that Jacques Fresco was the founding father for this initiative.

The Venus Project

The Venus project is based on the vision that we should organise ourselves in a global way. I join this vision. Well, I believe both: organize some things globally, but only the ones for which it is reasonable to do at that level. The majority is taken care of by local communities (cities, townships, etc.).

The Venus project takes science as the basis for creating an new economic model and implementation. Some main elements:

- Share the global resources in a reasonable way.
- Eliminate money.
- Use ICT and automation to free people.
- Produce in a eco-balance like way.

So, the RBE and Venus Project have - as far as I can see a similar bias.

Personally, I think the Venus project is the most sense full 'redesign' of our global ecology, which I have seen so far. This makes it very worth full.

I believe in the global orientation. I believe in eco balance (if you produce a product it should 'eat' the earth). I believe especially in leaving the system as we know it....

Of course I have some 'remarks' (additions). Do not see this as criticism. See it as synergy:

- I find the visions (video) pretty sterile Where are the people? Where is human expression? To people get happy of homes build by machines? Do we want to have 'big machines' growing our vegetables? I think I am not that kind of person.

- For me, the redesign should cover all ecological functions, like 'politics' (government / steering), justice, etc. I do not see (yet) how this arranged for in the Venus vision.

I believe both can be true: people building houses themselves, or let it do by machines. As long as people get more free time to do want they want. And I believe there are many people who want to be in the nature. Raise fruits and vegetables.

But I believe, that the essence of Venus is the right way: that ICT technology enables another implementation of (global) economy and society. And that it is *this* which make things far more efficient, or in other words: reduces the 'hidden loss'. That is why I believe in cooperation between the Novaglobe initiative and Venus Project, I believe we can create synergy, when we bring involved people, ideas and energy together. And offer the Novaglobe (in the Netherlands: Deniesa) community as a prototyping group. To let it work in a small group of people. Show what works and what does not work.

10.3.3 Transition Towns

Transition towns I see as places where people as much as possible keep money and pollution out: produce local, ecological, exchange service via 'natura swaps' "I paint your house, you grow my food".

From the Wikipedia: Transition Towns (also known as Transition network or Transition Movement) is a brand for environmental and social movements "founded (in part) upon the principles of permaculture", based originally on Bill Mollison's seminal Permaculture, a Designers Manual published in 1988. The Transition Towns brand of permaculture uses David Holmgren's 2003 book, Permaculture: Principles and Pathways Beyond Sustainability. These techniques were included in a student project overseen by permaculture teacher Rob Hopkins at the Kinsale Further Education College in Ireland. The term transition town was coined by Louise Rooney and Catherine Dunne. Following its start in Kinsale, Ireland it then spread to Totnes, England where Rob Hopkins and Naresh Giangrande developed the concept during 2005 and 2006. The aim of this community project is to equip communities for the dual challenges of climate change and peak oil. The Transition Towns movement is an example of socioeconomic localisation.

10.3.4 Ekosofia township – the Netherlands

Ekosofia is an initiative of a group of inspired people. They are creating a township with say about 50 to 100 people. This township is capable to produce its own food. A graphical representation:

Source: www.ekosofia.org

The ideas are open source, so feel free to contact the people!

An interesting thing I observed is the similarity in scape with the Venus project city design: A circular format with radial lines leading form the center outwards...

The main difference is that in the Ekosofia variant the work is done primary done by people, and within the Venus project the focus lies at machines doing the work. The idea in the Ekosofia township is that when everybody works for about half a day a week in the fields, it raises enough food for the township...

> *"Some day you'll return to*
> *Your valleys and your farms "*
>
> [Dire Straits, Brothers in Arms]

10.4 Already implemented <u>global</u> functions

10.4.1 A global function: Wikipedia

[Source WIkipedia] Wikipedia is a free, web-based, collaborative, multilingual encyclopedia project supported by the non-profit Wikimedia Foundation. Its 19 million articles (over 3.7 million in English) have been written collaboratively by volunteers around the world, and almost all of its articles can be edited by anyone with access to the site, but has only about 90,000 active contributors.[3][4] As of July 2011, there were editions of Wikipedia in 282 languages. Wikipedia was launched in 2001 by Jimmy Wales and Larry Sanger[5] and has become the largest and most popular general reference work on the Internet.

I find it interesting to note that there is some kind of governance and some kind of guidance. But that the far majority of the work is done by volunteers. And that the 'vehicle' underpinning it is a foundation, not a Ltd (see design chapter on Flowconomy as well).

10.4.2 A global function: Linux and Ubuntu

Linux and Ubuntu are so called 'open software' initiatives. Developers of all over the world contribute in making the software more stable, create applications (like open office) and keep it up to date.

Ubuntu I already use for about two years and more and more people around me use it too. Actually the whole Novaglobe book has been written on Ubuntu, using Open office Writer as text editor.

Microsoft needs billions and billions of dollars to create a equivalent (the Windows platform) and thus needs to ask a high price for users. Because Ubuntu has been developed without paying money to its developers it is free to use. And I consider it even to be better than Windows Vista...

An interesting thing to notice: Open software development has not the tendency to create a new version when there is no reason behind it. Microsoft does (to my opinion). The Windows Vista edition I -and many with me- consider to be a step backwards and just created and released because the company wants new license fees. A typical hidden loss gap and Iconomy dynamics.

We can learn a lot of open source software development. If we can apply the dynamics to other lines of 'business'... (food, care, banking, etc..). We make a huge step closer to the quantum leap upwards I feel.

10.4.3 A global function: Couchsurfing

Since about two years I am member of the couchsurfing community. The idea is simple: if available you can sleep at a 'couch' by somebody, and people can sleep at your couch as available. A nice example of the 'shareconomy' (sharing). And thus a Novaglobe example (it is already there!).

From the website:

"CouchSurfing is an international non-profit network that connects travelers with locals in over 230 countries and territories around the world. Since 2004, members have been using our system to come together for cultural exchange, friendship, and learning experiences. Today, over a million people who might otherwise never meet are able to share hospitality and cultural understanding.

Our mission as an organisation is to create inspiring experiences: cross-cultural encounters that are fun, engaging, and illuminating. These experiences take many forms. CouchSurfing's initial focus was on hosting and "surfing" (staying with a local as a guest in their home). Alongside these core experiences, we now also facilitate a growing array of activities and events.

We have a vision of a world where everyone can explore and create meaningful connections with the people and places they encounter. Each CouchSurfing experience shared by our members brings us closer to that vision."

See www.couchsurfing.org

I want to note some very interesting aspects:

1. I have never seen a robust and complete community infrastructure where people are real, and trust-ability is guaranteed to a high extent via all kinds of mechanisms (subscribe to the portal and you will see).
2. The community has created a practical 'government' structure via several stages: global, nation, city-hosts, etc. And this works.

10.5 Summary: When Venus meets Earth?

I feel the best direction is a combination of elements of the Venus project (mechanisation) and Transition / Ekosofia township like ideas (which I see as the more arts / earth oriented viewpoints). That is where the expression: "When earth meets Venus", is based upon. Find a mix between the science based direction, and an arts based direction (not meaning that one of the directions should give up their 'thing', they will exist *next* to each other, and are complementary). And I believe the application of information technology is crucial for make the global organisation work.

I think that a lot of people desire to work in the fields and create their food. And I believe information technology especially helps in our global organisation: resource allocation, communication, transport, pleasure, and our global Harmonicracy (peace, cooperation, etc.) function.

11 Synthesizing the main ecological functions

I have quite some experience with making 'governance' structures. Sounds strange but working at banks learned me this. A 'governance structure' is a structure how you want to organise a certain thing. That can be a change process, a group of people, a company, whatever. In my case it merely were 'change and implementation programmes': a certain thing had to change in the bank's organisation and ICT landscape. The question was how to connect all those involved people, stakeholders, etc. in such a manner that the bank would not break down implementing the desired change, and that we would achieve the change at the desired date against desired costs (and risks).

But creating a 'governance structure' for a whole world is quite something different. But let's try. It is only a design, a proposal, which can be improved or changed, once somebody puts new idea on top of it, or the world changes...

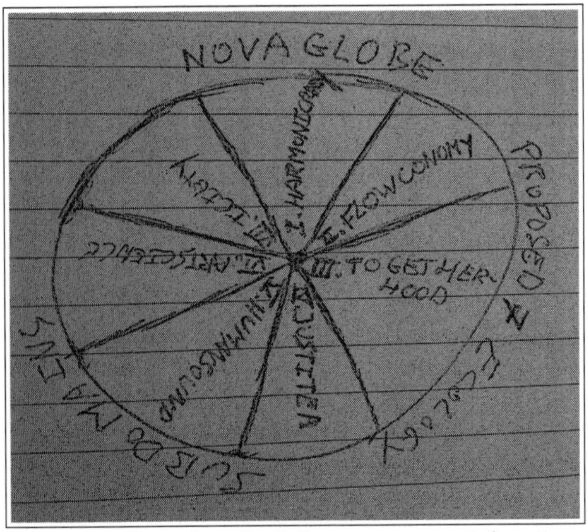

Figure: A first sketch of the seven eco subdomains.

Seven is the 'holy number' and it is the number which is seen as the maximum 'span off control' in managers land. So, I decided to try to come to seven main ecological areas. "Eco subdomains" I call them. I did quite some 'research': Reading books of other writers their views on how 'government departments' should be organised. And of course I have been analyzing and watching already existing structures. The main problem was that I had to size down the number of departments. Trying this, I got the feeling I didn't have the good names for the newly arising areas. So I created new names. Why not?

Another very important advantage of creating new names is that already existing departments and organisations are not placed as a whole in a newly defined area. Which I explicitly do not want to happen. We rebuild the system, remember?

And it hopefully opens the minds of many people, to start wondering on the new world. How we could do things. How we can create our own heaven on earth. Or at least migrate on step closer to it. I came to the following main areas. I will discuss each area later on in more depth. With these elaborations I also want to make clear *why* it makes sense to me to pick these seven 'boundaries' and not others... The seven main ecological areas in Novaglobe are:

Eco subdomains of Novaglobe:

1. Harmonicacy
2. Flowconomy
3. Togetherhood
4. Artscience
5. Humansound
6. Justitia
7. Iciety

The seven eco subdmains at a glance

(In following chapters each subdomain will be elaborated in more detail).

I - Harmonicracy

Harmonicracy is the equivalent of present 'politics' and 'government'. The requirement behind it is 'a subsystem which takes care of a minimal of organisation of the ecology'. I do not believe in total anarchy. I have been watching the current political system and came to the conclusion that the 'party based' system is far over its top. It is nor neither democratic neither not-corrupt nor efficient in a pure sense. It was the maximum change at that time the world could do (about around 1850), when the power of the kings and religion was broken. And there was no information technology. And many people couldn't even read. But times have changed, and political system walks on its last legs due to over rulement and never ending growth of its employees And, maybe the most important: a far more beautiful alternative is available. Mainly thanks to ICT. We can now go back that the original roots of politics, politeia:

Politeia, the original word for politics, stands for **organizing** the maximum **harmonic** society. The opposite of politeia is idiotes (Greek). Idiotes translated to english give 'egoism'.

Idiots I see as the present implementation of our political system. An Egocracy.

See the crushing parallel with present politics: individuals are mostly egoists. And parties themselves serve their own goals over cooperation for countries sake. Even if a fellow party has a good proposal it will be torpedo-ed by another party, because it is afraid the 'crowd' will see that another party made up a good plan. Better sabotage it. Yeahh.

So Politeia stands for both the political system and steering by the 'government'.

II - Flowconomy

Flowconomy can be seen as the equivalent of economy. Or in other words:

Flowconomy is the subsystem taking care of the creation and exchange of goods and services.

De word 'flow' directly expresses the essences: leave the value chain free as possible. So: minimal taxes on the flow. Minimal regulations on the flow. Let people exchange

things in between them. Do not fuzzle with it with all kinds of rules. And if possible: create *guidelines* instead of rules...
Within the Flowconomy the required value generation for the 'common desire' is integrated (a thing we what we nowadays call tax). It is very important to integrate those two, to avoid two distinctive tax and economy departments pulling at the same thing. Like we have nowadays.

And: Within the Flowconomy, no lending, no non-proporational money creation, no intrinsic inflation, no (companies) with stock shares. Note: value chains in the Flowconomy can exists next to value chains in the economy...

III - Togetherhood

This function is about arranging those structures, guidelines, processes, etc. to arrange the living together of people in a more harmonic fashion. At a 'micro' scale (say 1 to 50 people), up to the whole world. It is recognised that it is important to try to bring back a 'human scale'. And to bring back a family feeling of 'earlier days': children, middle agers and elderly people together. In little settings. But without the pressure which probably made many people to escape their parents place as soon as they can drive a car.

> *"The Iconomy benefits from separating people as much as possible on the smallest amount of square feet"*

The present system separates children in crèches and schools. Elderly in elderly pensions. And people who 'cracked' in mental institutes. If possible with large number at the same time and place, fulfilling the 'economy of scale' rule. And you could say that the 'working' people are separated at day in their offices. Strange to observe that we only use 50% of our buildings potential: during daytime our houses are empty, and during night time the offices. What a waste of goods... idiotery.

And the 'middle agers' and fit people drive as lunatics to get from one place to the other. From school to their parents, to the crèche, to work, through the traffic jam, to children parties at the other side of the city. Not noticing they bring themselves (and their children) a step closer towards entering an mental institution each day themselves due to a mental breakdown... ADHD, depressed? Yeahh right, you find it strange people get sick? I don't. We should give society a curing pill, not the people...

IV - Artscience

Why is art so important? And why combining it with science, which is a highly rational discipline? Art is about expression. Art is about earth. About making contact with once senses. The best way to find your vocale, to what you are here for on earth it to make contact with that same earth. And painting, making music, drawing, sporting and enjoying these expressions[20] as a 'observer' is the way. We have forgotten that. I was forgotten that. Why did I break down when I couldn't climb anymore (due to having a mortgage, a child and rebuilding a house at the same moment)? I believe it (sporting, feeling the rocks, nature) was my recharger of all those bad energy which I got from working in the banking industry all those years. The 'problem' with the heart things is that we cannot proof it with the head. So we rationalise that domain out of our world...

20 More in general we could say 'creating something with our body'. My mother gets her relief from working in the garden...

And it was after my suicide attempt I released how insane narrow focused my profession had become: I was specialist in banking, specialised in financial reporting, mortgages and Basel II, intending to specialise on 'securitisation' deals and underlying balance sheets and accounting rules. This I find spirit killing nowadays. We have become over specialised. Why? Again because of economic mechanisms which make us to super specialise, in order to have the best curriculum vitae in a certain niche. This is the only way for all. If you do not follow this working class rule, the system will ditch you. Simple as that. Survival of the fittest. Not of the most sense full.

And this, while I believe society needs people who can combine all kinds of disciplines. Who see the relations. Alchemists we need. See what is really happening in this world. But the harder we push our eyes to the 'looking hole', the less we see... and thus so few people see what is really happening in the (I/e)conomy. And why. And even more... what we can do about it. So many people trapped in a tunnel vision which I was too.

And only the combination of emotion and logic. Left and right brain part, spirilogic, can bring us to the wisdom we need to bring us out of this jamming world.

V - Humansound

Humansound is the equivalent of physical and mental care. Its foundation lies in the combination of the more 'spiritual' ways of viewing (like Buddhism) and nowadays emerging visions based on quantum physics. The nice thing is that they come together. The bad thing is that the 'industry' (Iconomy) does not like this. Because many companies and systems are based on a more physical oriented thinking (like pharmacy). And in addition our care systems have evolved more and more to a 'repair and break' state: physicians do not benefit from a world without patients. The same for dentists if there are not teeth which get wholes in it. And this is nobodies guilt, this is a consequence of our present economic social structures, and system dynamics and of course the Primary Iconomy Constructors.

So why create ways of life and methods which *really* cure physical and mental problems? Because these things do not get the big money. These things are even sabotaged (like fuel efficient solutions are sabotaged in automotive industry). That is why the Flowconomy underground is so important: as long as we have a profit driven Iconomy, our care systems will evolve more and more worse. Simple as that.

Because the roots on which they are build do not take societies and peoples health and happiness as focus, but power, money, ego and market share.

VI - Justitea

The sixth area is dedicated to judge behaviour in 'good' and 'bad'. And more important to help creating a society in which people do less and less feel the incentive to do 'bad'. This area is called 'Justitea' instead of 'justice'. The different name seems to be a minor detail, but what is intended is to give a 'feminine' feeling.

> ***Lady Justice*** *(Latin: Justitia), the Roman goddess of Justice, who is equivalent to the Greek goddess Dike, is an allegorical personification of the moral force in judicial systems*

The stories about criminals not getting their 'treatment' because of a juridical procedure failure are too many. Too many are also the stories in which a victim gets a more worse treatment than the offender.

The reason for this? Too many rules. Too many laws. The whole system has become too complex. And lawyers and judges benefiting from endless lawsuits (money). I often think that my 4yold daughter is more capable of speaking justice than lawyers and the judges. The system has been rationalised. At typical male treat to do. But the feeling has gone. And combined with the principles of Iconomy: does a judge benefits from less crimes? No. Does a lawyer benefits from less 'cases'? No. So where does the whole system tends to after enough years of enlarging and adjusting it? Endless lawsuits, an a more worse and worse system. Which cannot be changed. Unless -here too- we take out the PICS. A lawyer working for 300 euro's an hour? Insane! That is an amount the ordinary maybe can spend monthly. On hour layer time. And this should bring a more harmonic society? Begin with you self and ask only a humble fee. Idiots.

Only recreating as system for justice will help.

This is what we intend for. And keep it simple. And make smart use of the Internet. In the new system criminals can escape a prison, but cannot escape Internet... principles as used within couch surfing (trusted) communities will be applied as well within the Novaglobe Justitea system.

Within the Netherlands the council which goes over guidelines over privacy (which is highly related to the Justice department in the Netherlands) wants to put a penalty of about 25.000 euro's on putting a photo of a burglar on the web. Iconomy at work. And if this justice department was capable of solving criminal cases.. I just read an article that hardly and thefts are solved by the police and justice departments. But I know why they want to forbid it.. it will proof that crime figures will drop when criminals are made transparent on the web. And that will make them loose their jobs, and money.

A thing I believe is that a criminal loses his right on privacy when he commits a crime, respect goes over privacy.

> Within the Netherlands the council which goes over guidelines over privacy (which is highly related to the Justice department in the Netherlands) wants to put a penalty of about 25.000 euro's on putting a photo of a burglar on the web.
>
> A thing I believe is that a criminal loses his right on privacy when he commits a crime, respect goes over privacy.

Another advantage: corrupt police officers in certain countries cannot make advantage of their position an be bribed. The Internet is accessible for all... Just make things transparent... in a respectful manner.

VII - Iciety

The seventh area is dedicated to the newest development in our world: ICT. Iciety stands for ICT - Society. It stands for all kinds of mechanisms, group forming, interaction with the internet (but mobile telecom as well) having as a basis. ICT can be seen as a thread. But it is an opportunity as well. The design of Novaglobe as stated in this book would not be feasible without the usage of ICT. As stated in the Venus (also feminine???) as well, ICT gives us a mighty Ring of Power (for those knowing Lord of the Rings books from Tolkien). But if used wrongly devastation can be extremely huge as well. As we see actually nowadays by the devastation which hedge funds create, and the enormous ruins created by financial derivatives -which mortgages can be accounted to as well- would not have been possible without the aid of ICT.

So, high time to stop abusing this in potential beautiful element for bad things, and start using it (more) for good things. I want to note that a lot of beautiful good things already happen via ICT and on the world wide web... see for instance what kind of connections Twitter brings together, or Facebook.

The coming seven chapters are dedicated to elaborate the design per eco subdomain in more detail.

12 Eco subdomain I – Harmonicracy

This chapter is about how to organise our 'government' and 'steering' in a more sense full way. Together with the Flowconomy I consider the Harmonicracy as one of the two most important Eco subdomains to be redefined and reimplemented.

12.1 Analysis

First take a look at present political systems:

- The good thing is that it provides in a manner of steering which is pretty not corrupt-able (dictator taking over), nor that one 'party' has the power: religion, monarchy, etc.

There are disadvantages as well:

- It so very **inefficient**: In the Netherlands each four year the whole board is changed. And often each board undoes the activities of the previous board. There is no company nor foundation I know which replaces its whole board each four year... billions of euro's wasted.
- It badly **expressing** its citizens: in the Netherlands we have Internet based tools to help to choose your party (already a sign at the wall we need it), based on your opinion on 40 main topics. Many times I get a party advised which is certainly not *my* party. And often I ask myself: why not take the outcome of all

those main topics, and see this as the will of the people, and take that as one of the input for a government plan?

- **Political parties** are strange things: I often say, "I want the organisational power of the *right*, combined with the ideas of *left*". And what does right and left say? I feel that parties are an expression of the 'system' (Iconomy, again) to divide and conquer. It does make no sense anymore. The main thing parties do is battling each others, causing for billions of loose, only already in the Netherlands. And I still don't grasp the difference between 'Republicans' and 'Democrats'... the USA seems to have a two party system, which leaves hardly any space for innovation (via a new party). As a voter you don't have much to choose from I feel. And than the way people vote: "Yeahh, I like party X, but they are so small, I can better vote for party Z..". Idiotery. It is meant to bring to expression what people want, no?

So, -especially with the usage of ICT-, can't we do better than that?

12.2 Requirements

Thinking about what this 'subsystem should do' I came to the following:

1. Provide for a **maximum harmonic society** for its citizens, in harmony with the earth. Leading to some derived requirements:
2. Be **robust** against people or parties which want to take the 'power'.
3. Do it **efficient**. Meaning that a minimal of human hours, money, earth, etc. is spoiled or used.

4. Make sure every soul **has a voice** in the 'combined plan' government.

I also added some observations:

5. **Reason weighed voting.** If you are pro referenda, take a look at opportunistic referenda in eg. California where the government cannot organise the country because there is always 70% of the people against a certain measure. People decide only on that certain topic, and do not take other topics in consideration. Therefore I would like a system where when one's statement **is more reasonable**, the bigger the chance it is put to practice. This asks people to *think* about solutions, or delegate this to others. This also is something different than we have at this moment: I have send many emails to parties, ministers, etc. None of them answered. The whole political systems seems jammed with talking and beating each other... I would like politicians to listen to the people and ask '**why** are you voting against... etc'.

6. Looking at many politicians we have nowadays: I would like to have the **wisest and goodest** people at the steering wheel. Not the ones which can shout the loudest or use the weapons of the media and propaganda in the most evil way (survival of the fittest, it almost just like fighting and war). I want the goodest and wisest to survive, often these people even do not *want* to be in the political arena. So we should create a system which facilitates this. How? Replace the arena, which is a battle place, by a harmonic place... a place of reason and harmony, so that the people of whom we want them to lead us feel attracted to be there.

Looking at present system - in most western countries- I conclude only requirements 1 and 2 are met. If you think you have a voice in the present system... try to get a certain solution on the agenda... try! The system gives you the *feeling* you have influence, but your voice is battered and mingled in such way it is hardly heard, and probably misunderstood when it reaches the rooms of those steering our society.

12.3 Design, can we do it differently?

On the word 'Harmonicracy'

Suggestion proposal during 13 August 2011 Novaglobe symposium, by Johannes Heimrath (Club of Budapest) on the **word** 'harmonicracy'. Johannes states that 'cracy' is not a nice word to use (meaning rule or power). He is right on this. He suggests a word like 'archi' at the end, having a different bias. This would make the word 'Harmoniarchi' or 'harmoniarchy'. At a next symposium we will further decide on this subject. Another proposal is something like 'harmoniart' (arts of harmony), by Don Willard. Maybe in between new inspiration comes up anywhere on the world where people read this book... all input is welcome, please send it to contact@novaglobe.org

---Remember the next sections is all is 'only' a proposal!---

For me there are two things which I want to have in place, as a citizen:

1. That people represent my stake which I can trust (are good people), and who have the 'best' talents and experience to do so. I name this the *people-aspect*.

2. That things I want or the ideas that I have are heard, and answered in a reasonable way. I name this the *topic-aspect.*

Combined with the earlier stated requirements, I do not see the reason why why should have a board that is replaced each four year.

Having a board replaced each four your is not reasonable

Thinking about the 40-points voting tool, and looking at environments as www.digg.com, I see a completely different solution. Which I call 'Harmonicracy'. It consists of the following main elements:

1. A mechanism to choose our primary organisers at different levels. These people have especially organizing skills.
2. A mechanism to identify the most important *topics* and having discussion on them, moderated by subject matter experts.
3. A House of representatives consisting of 49 members. It consists of the steering team and six councils. These people are selected by voting bottom up. This house has the formal 'power'.
4. A Conscious council, consisting of popular artists and scientists. This council selects new members itself and has no formal power in operational affairs

12.3.1 Selecting the steering team members (People-aspect)

First, the people which do steer us. Imagine that we do it like this (inspired on how I think it would work in the earlier days with less people and 'clans' or little villages):

1. Each year a voting takes place to select a new

member for the national steering team (via his way it is refreshed every seven years).

2. Every citizen is member of a group of 30 to 49 members (49 = 7x7). Most logically these groups are formed on the location where people reside. With the usage of ICT this is easy to arrange.

3. Each group appoints it representer (by some sort of selecting procedure).

4. Each representer is member of a group of 30 to 49 representatives (level II).

5. Each of these groups selects one representer out of their midst. Resulting in the level III steering members..

6. Etc, etc.

In the Netherlands with about 17 million inhabitants, we need only about five layers to end up with seven steering team members. That feels like less 'levels' than we have nowadays.

In the national steering team no member can stay longer than seven years. Each year a member is replaced. This steering team gives steering to national organisation.

Maybe we can call all these representatives 'hooders'. Or we can create another name. And maybe these people are also the people for bringing justice or do mediation when people within a group have a 'dispute'.

A graphical sketch looks like this (in the sketch also the different councils are depicted as well as the topic forum, see next sections).

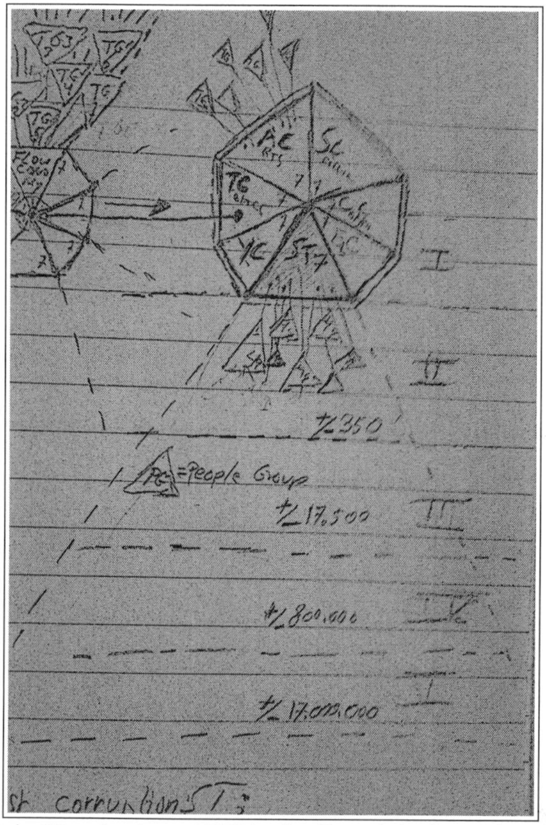

Sketch: Steering team (ST7 in the figure), in the midst of six councils (septagram at the top). And the five layers required to choose the delegates. In the left you see the TopicGroup topology (see further in next section).

12.3.2 Topic Fora (Topic-aspect)

The topic for a work as follows:

1. Everybody can post a topic / issue on certain Internet for a. These for a are coupled to

TopicGroups (or a new topic group is started).

2. Each topic group has a steer team of seven people maximum.
3. Direct or indirectly the TopicGroups are connected to one of the seven Eco subdomains.
4. If applicable the steering team chair passes through the outcome of a discussion (rationalisation) on a certain theme up warts until it reaches the House of Delegates. If a topic has only local relevance, it is taken care of locally (and the outcome is shared with other localities).

12.3.3 House of Representatives

To my opinion the operational steering group should not be bigger than the size which might fit in a big living room. A parliament with 100+ member I think will create bureaucracy. Therefore I propose a size of 49 members. And I propose to abandon the party system as we have known until know, which is mainly replaced by the TopicGroups (content side) and people delegation model.

However, I see in the Netherlands a tendency that people identify themselves with certain communities: elderly, the young and ICT driven, spirituals, etc. Therefore I suggest a 'community' council in the House of Representatives. For me the following categories make the most sense (at this moment).

1. Steering team (seven members)
2. Elderly council (seven members)
3. Youngsters council (seven members)
4. Communities council (seven members)
5. Topics council (seven members)

6. Artists council (seven members)
7. Scientists council (seven members)

All these councils refresh each seven year totally and with a pace of one member per year. Selecting new members is probably done the same way as the steering team is being selected (via sub councils).

The Topics council is crewed with experts on certain areas. 3 positions are reserved for people coming from the 'institutes', 3 seats are reserved for people who gained there expertise from practice.

The idea is that the proposed concept aligns as smoothly as possible with already existing movements, parties, etc. Representatives from these movements just have to take part in one of the groups within the Harmonicracy, to get there voice heard. They can just keep there own identity and way of organisation.

Some practical notes:

1. A measure to improve **robustness** is that if 2/3 of the House of Representatives votes for dismantling the steering team, this will happen immediately, and new steering team members will be chosen. This goes for layer two as well (350 people). I decided to explicitly not create a referendum option that say by a 2/3 vote of all people the steering team must go. This will introduce populistic steering, at that is something we don't want anymore. People have influence via choosing their delegates (and TopicGroups).

2. On **salaries and time**. I don't feel it is a good idea to have full time politicians again. I propose that House of Delegates get only a fee of 2000 euro's a month and in return they should be available two days a week for meetings. Still being a member in

society (in whatever 'occupation') is a pre to be elected in the House. Let's try this model and see if it works within the Novaglobe (associated) community. Because we keep thinks much more simple, we don't have to talk and read as much paperwork as nowadays politicians...

12.3.4 Consciousness Council

I believe it is a good thing that those people with the less desire for formal power lead us. And that it is high time feminine energy (can be men too) go over the direction where to go. And at least there is more heart in it and less ratio.

Sketch of the Conscious Council, supporting the house of representatives.

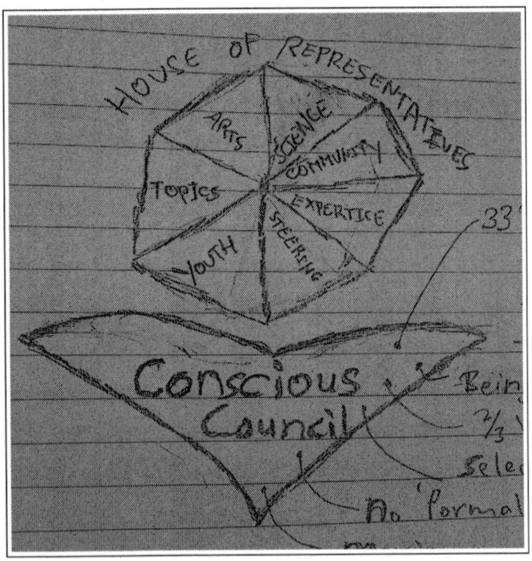

That led me to artists.

Than I thought: "Imagine that popular artists join in a sort of council and make a voice together, or would steer us". Well, one thing I learned about artists: in general they detest politics and do detest being In a sort of structure. And in addition I hardly know artists who proof to be strong organisers.

That made me decide we should separate a group of organisers (that became the steering team), and a thing a became to call 'conscious council'.

Ans already about three years ago I saw Ervin Laszlo came to a same sort of model: he joined artists and scientists in a global group (Club of Budapest and Wisdom Council). It is all not that formal, but together they have a huge influence (think of members such as Peter Gabriel, Deepak Chopra, and even the Dalai Lama is related).

A next question: imagine we create such a council: how are the members selected? And what about refreshing the council? And does it have formal power, can it dismantle the House of Representatives for instance? After many, many hours of elaboration I decided to propose:

- That this council asks its own new members, and decides itself wish members go.
- Has a maximum size of 33 members.
- Has a facilitating member.
- Has no formal power.
- Longest duration for a member is 17 years.
- Each year two members come and go.

This council will be interwoven in a topology of global councils, this topology I propose to name 'CouncilGallery' (like al gallery of councils). The relation of these councils will set in a organic manner. The Harmonicracy subdomain takes care of maintaining the topology and make it transparent via the web.

Maybe for this we should make some guidelines as well, as saying that each council can relate to at max 7 other councils.

The idea on this is that when the Global Conscious Council is not supported anymore by the other councils, it will sink automatically and another council will pop up which Is better equipped for its task. This is open source dynamics. At it is not a 'shame' when this happens, it is good. Within Novaglobe it is not anymore about competition, it is about letting the proper things and people flow to their most proper place for themselves and society.

How does It has influence: imagine what happens when this council communicates it does not support the House of Representatives anymore, and gives its support to other (new) members? I see a high chance the House of Representatives decides to dismantle the steering team...

Some final proposed requirements:

- 2/3 of this council consists of **women**[21].
- 2/3 of the council consists of (the most) **popular** artists. Being popular means influence, simple as that.
- Being an **artists *and* scientist** is a pre (is science not arts as well?).
- The council **meets** both at 'gatherings' (like festival symposia, say two times a year) as in a more informal fashion.

---

[21](I know: it is about feminine energy, but as long as we cannot measure that we go for what we can see. And I know: typical woman achieving the highest positions in business are more typical 'man' than the men surrounding her. But that is in the Iconomy, within the Flowconomy, Novaglobe it is about 'goodness' of person. Not its toughness, or topical competitive and populistic skills.

12.4 Further definitions, processes and putting it to action

I realise that creating a new 'government-political' model is not something you do easily. It is not for nothing that the present constitution and procedures easily make up 1000 pages I think.

But, at the other hand, if we don't just start, it certainly will not change. And more and more I feel we only think it has to be very complex. Simplification is the key. Keep it simple.

My proposal it to just start doing it within the Novaglobe (associated) community, and see what happens. If required adjust the model along the line. In such way the model can grow as the community and its relevance grows...

13 Eco subdomain II – The Flowconomy

As stated earlier, I consider the Flowconomy -as alternative economy implementation- together with the Harmonicracy as one of the two most important eco subdomains to be redesigned.

13.1 Introduction

13.1.1 Free flow and modesty

The kernel of the new ecosystem is based on '**enabling free flow**'. We will eliminate all rules, constitutions, habits, concepts, which are in fact not necessary. And which hinder free flow of goods and people. And flow is not only about a geographical flow, it certainly is also about the potential to change: that a person can change, a thing can change, etc. Sot the Flowconomy is achieving **freedom**.

And it is about **modesty** don't take more of the world or

other people than you need. People seem to have lost track on how to apply modesty in western world. Again: Iconomy and modesty are not combinable. The Beast only wants economic growth, and makes us want it too...

"Live simple, sot that others may simply live" [Mahatma Ghandi]

And we will abandon the destructive elements of competition. The Flowconomy will have far less 'Hidden Loss Gaps'. And, for the criticisers saying it is Utopia... it already exist: look at the Wikipedia, look at Linux and open software development...

13.1.2 Antroposophy and associations

And a last interesting thing to note here: for those familiar with anthroposophy (with Rudolph Steiner as one as the most well know persons): the Flowconomy implementation might proof to be the same as proposed economy concepts. You can see the Wikipedia als a global association[22] for the function 'encyclopedia'. You can see the open source conglomerate around Linux/Ubuntu as an global association for the function 'operating system'. Etcetera.

I tried to find a practical way on how we could already put the Flowconomy to action, without for instance having to adjust legislation (which easily can take up to five years). And I tried to find a model which can co-exist next to the Iconomy. You can read more on this in the last section 'Putting it to action'.

13.1.3 Freed from desire

Take a look at these song lyrics:

---

[22] If interested, I advise you to read two thin books by Herbert Witzenman, named 'The Just Price' and his book on 'Social Organics". Both books will be obtainable via Willehalmpress (www.willehalmpress.org) outerly the end of 2011.

"My love has got no money
He's got his strong beliefs
My love has got no power
He's got his strong beliefs
My love has got no fame
He's got his strong beliefs
My love has got no money
He's got his strong beliefs

Want more and more
People just want more and more
Freedom and love
What he's looking for
Want more and more
People just want more and more
Freedom and love
What he's looking for

Freed from desire
Mind and senses purified
Freed from desire
Mind and senses purified
Freed from desire
Mind and senses purified

Freed from desire

Nanana..."

[Freed from desire, Gala]

Essence of the song, maybe:

Bring in mind the Goodvalues chapter as beliefs. And bring in mind the idea of modesty an seeing 'heaven' as 'have non'... I hope I become or am like the 'love' described in this song: "My love has got no money, but he's got his strong beliefs". And I try to live like this for three years, and I think that my senses and mind more and more become purified on what the real essence of life is about. For me it is not about money, showing of with material goods, etc. It is living your essence (sense) and your strong beliefs (goodvalues, or your own set of values), act as your beacens... These seven goodvalues act as my rational compass. My emotions act as my emotional compass...

And recall the section on the 'Flipped Maslow' pyramid.

13.2 From aggregating material to letting it flow

Currency (money) literary means 'flow'. See the chapter on money as well. Money should be facilitated maximally to flow. The phenomenon to aggregate money is in that sense a not-good thing. This, in contradiction to what our bankers, economists, retirement funds and government want us to believe. People aggregating their money is something which is especially good for these institutes them, they parasite on your money. 'Save to last'... well the recent breaking down of retirement funds is a good example that this is a fiction...

And why is it, actually, that we people believe it is good to aggregate as much money as possible 'for later'? The reason is twofold:

1. Fear
2. More and more expensive life standards

We have fear that we might up into a shortage of money. And this is combined with the second reason: expensive life standards: we want to have a big house all for ourselves. Drive a -at maximum three year old- car. Eat expansive. Have money for the newest electronics, etc. (see the section on the Flipped Maslov Pyramid).

Yes, in that case the standard social care facility might not be enough.

In the Netherlands, each inhabitant older than say 65 gets a monthly 'elderly social security', consisting of about 800 to 1000 euro's a month. If you hire a room for say about 400 euro's, this should be enough to live a good life. I think.

But no, we want more. We are not so modest....

And all the bills become a burden. An obligation. And so we trade our so desired freedom for a cage. Our luxuries and material stuff. "All that glitters is gold" (Stairwary to heaven song, Led Zeppelin).

If we just arrange that we can live on our standard welfare payments, we don't need parasiting retirement funds and banks. These institutes are the same which push us into all kinds of obligations and fear us with their retirement fund advisers... best lesson for the salesman: make sure the client gets fear (or desire), than show the goods...

Why are retirement funds breaking down? Because they started to try to gain money on money. 'Investments' they call it. And more and more expensive staff came to work at the funds. And to pay all these staff, the funds need to take bigger and bigger risks to be able to have a chance on the desired profits.

But the sky is not the limit, and risks now come to reality.

Retirement funds are breaking down, and leave people in without their illusion of a rich old day. All the money given to retirement funds can be considered to be thrown away.

Why this elaboration on this example (retirement funds)? To illustrate the sense of two important orientations of the Flowconomy:

1. An orientation of not-having / **modesty**, in other words: a focus more on the spiritual, non material aspect than we have nowadays in the western world. From 'have' we go to 'be'. I do not need to ***have*** a house to live in it. I don't need to *have* a guitar to play on it. Etcetera.

2. An orientation on **flow**: to make visible how useless it is to not let for example the money flow to new creations, new added value. Instead we put it in retirement funds and on saving accounts...

13.3 From having to guardianship

About a new implementation of 'having': as long as the goods I want around me are available, things are fine.... And when other people simply respect that a certain guitar is with me, the 'effect' will be the same as when you would posses it. But using different words -and really feeling that you are only a guardian- of the goods make a huge difference...

And having things gives a burden. Are anchors for your being. When you want to move geographically you have to carry it all around. Sometimes, when I look at all those goods when people move, I get a vision of Hobbits (again), those little people of the Lord in the Rings books, living in their holes. And aggregating lots and lots of stuff. Precious goodies...And with each birthday we get more goodies. Mostly goodies which we don't need. But, yes, habits are habits. No, hobbits?

Example of the Flowconomy: Giving ritual

Cora Scherp, a friend and change maker, recently told me that Indians had a 'give' ritual. Within that culture it was a usual thing to pass goods, even if used. Or maybe especially when used (the spirit of the previous 'owners') is in the good. This is typically a Flowconomy aspect: why not give away things you don't want or use anymore? Why is it, that in Western countries all things we give as a present for example should be new? Why is used not good enough anymore? Why is it that children want new goods at birthdays?

Because the Iconomy, the beast, has made us crazy. With all its commercials (again: watch the Zeitgeist Moving Forward movie). And because it is hardly possible to create profit out of the re-use business. As long as plundering the earth, and making new products is cheaper than re-using materials... and as long as the primary Iconomy constructors are in place, this will not change...

Do not worry: in Novaglobe you don't have to abandon all your goods. Each of us is challenged to find the golden means for her or him. How to live in abundance. Which things to share with who, and which things to keep for your own... our world is not about black and white... and it would help a lot it if we could seed 'Flowconomy constructors': base elements which motivate people and communities to share and re-use things, and live more modest.

13.4 Some examples

13.4.1 Flowconomy and RBE example: Liftbus

Like many of us, I have spent quite some time wondering on how to bring a solution for the present transportation system: we want to take public transportation to a higher level. But at the same hand: a metro, or bus does not give the advantages of a car: which can be guided to a very specific place at a very specific time (especially railway leaves big areas unreachable).

When I was hitchhiking my way to France I had an insight, when I was watching all those -mostly empty- cars pass my wanting thumb...

I thought: "Actually, **the supply** is already there... at each moment a car is driving -with space left in- in the direction I want, even to very specific and desolate places. The only thing is how to bring demand and supply together". Why don't we?

A main reason for not doing this is 'haste': we don't have time to stop. But two other important reasons are that drivers **simply don't know** that somebody just living next door want to go the same direction. And people do not trust other people... hitchhiking has become rare in the Netherlands. A strange thing from social perspective.

So, what we could do in Novaglobe is to create solutions to really make better usage of the supply of transportation already there. And it is possible, and not so difficult. Only neither government neither the business parties want to stimulate this, because it is gonna cost them or GDP (government) or profit (business). And again, nothing happens in the good direction in the Iconomy. Even worse: new developments and legislation make things only worse: insurance companies prohibit truck drivers to take hitchhikers. Hitchhiking along highways gets forbidden (which makes sense, not to hitchhike next to the fast lane, bit than, make special -sensible- hitch hike points). Iconomy in action.

And, with ICT we can arrange for a trust and connecting supply and demand. All information is already there, almost all people enter there destination in their car navigator. Only facilitate these people to share this information with the Liftbus community. Easily. Why wait? Why not put this to action. Within the Novaglobe social media infrastructure we aim to put this to action.

And about the name 'Liftbus': in ICT terms a 'bus' is a concept which is shared by multiples processes. These processes (like applications like Word) can ask questions to that bus. The bus takes care of an efficient resource allocation. And of course bus stands for the bus (as a car), sharing one vehicle with more people

And the attention full reader will have noticed that this concept is a clear example of the Resource Based Economy, promoted by the Zeitgeist movement. A thing I want to make clear is that fundamental world changing solution lie often directly under our nose, often realizable via simplification of things instead of making things more complex or introducing new infrastructure and so.

13.4.2 Keep ideas free foundation

The present 'anti economy' avoids a lot of good ideas to find their way to reality. The reason is that these ideas might 'cost' profit (even if the ideas are good tor our environment), or certain 'people' are afraid of loosing power.

So, these people or institutions just 'buy' the idea. The inventor is rich till he dies, but the world is deprived from another good idea. Once the idea is 'bought' it gets patented and nobody can use it. Iconomy games.

A way to keep ideas free for the open source dynamics is to create a foundation together in which inventors can 'store' their idea. The foundation takes care of getting all kinds of patents in every nation of the world. Via some kind of 'just price' model the inventor gets an fair reward, like a base income to be able to continue is workings. The required money could be made by letting 'Iconomy' companies pay for the ideas, ideally the Flowconomy parties can use ideas for free. This seems fair to me, because if the Iconomy would not 'steal' this ideas and let them free, the invetors did not have to protect them from certain Iconomy actors...

13.4.3 Make things work on 12V

Did you ever notice how many voltage adapters you have in your house? And how much annoyance, pollution and costs this brings? In terms of materials but in terms of transforming energy voltages as well. And ever thought of *why* industry does not standardise?

It is all because of Iconomy games, again. There are as far as I know no significant technical reasons. Vendors like it that once your adapter breaks down, you have to buy a new one, or even buy a complete new mobile phone for instanec. Vendors like it that you have to stay with their products and their specific adapter sockets and voltages. Complete idiotery.

One time, when I was thinking about the electricity scheme for a music studio I was making, I thought: "Maybe I should make a secondary electricity network on 12V, next to the 'normal' 220V (which is the base voltage in the Netherlands". Than I started to wonder why this was not a 'normal' thing to do when we are building houses:

- I think energy loss is limited because you make one central transformer per house (the reason why we use high voltage is that this gives less energy leakage during transport).
- No chance anymore on electrocution (especially for children).
- No need for endless adapters anymore.
- Electric applications used in our house can be used in our cars as well (computers, hifi, kitchen stuff, etc.), because cars are already standardised on 12V batteries.

Why not?

PS: www.whynot.net I find to be an extremely interesting website. Maybe we can promote this platform to be the main point as our source for new ideas with Novaglobe (instead of heaving to fetch ideas spread over numerous websites...).

13.5 Communistic or capitalistic?

A response often get is: "Well, this sounds like communism, we don't want that!". My answer: maybe 'social liberality' comes close. Can you please tell me what you define as 'communism'?

That word has been corrupted by power driven dictators in the previous Sow-jet union, and other communistic countries. The Flowconomy model is a synthesis of the goof things of communism and the good things of capitalism. It creates a 'golden means'. The negative elements of the two models are where possible eliminated. But you cannot say whether is is capitalistic or communistic. It is Flowconomy, a model on its own.

In a nutshell the *good* aspects of **communism** (and than communism in the pure sense) is the intention to do things together, share goods and to take care for each other. The *negative* (realisation) was that it resulted in a planned economy by the government, not leaving space for individual entrepreneurship, very narrow individual freedom and a low degree of efficiency (hidden unemployment). And the stress caused by a repressive and controlling government.

The *good* things of **liberal capitalism** in a nutshell are the freedom of the individual, incentive for renewal, or creation of new and more efficient things, and a certain degree of social care system. The *negative* (trend) is more and more apathetic and self oriented and more and more frightened people, increasing pressure to perform, an enormous percentage of people suffering from 'mental diseases' (even our youth). And a decreasing feeling of living a life which makes sense, because we have to work so hard and to the things the 'system' wants us to do.

System dictatorship

A thing which is worth mentioning is that both systems seem to be more and more a dictatorship. A dictatorship by the system (and most rich and powerful people) and some kind of plan economy. Even in Western countries as the Netherlands the government is more and more dictating the economy. In both systems we see a increasing government staff working force which occupies itself with controlling, steering and the suppressing of her citizens. In the previous East Germany (DDR) it was the Stasi, now in the Netherlands it is the tax agency and the social services departments. I feel.

Recently a friend -who had been living in Berlin- told me that some DDR inhabitants desired more and more for the days when they still lived in a communistic regime. The materialistic liberalism also brings a lot of misery.

We now know.

13.6 Iconomy , Communism and Flowconomy

In the table below, you'll find some important aspects to classify the three different systems (nowadays Capitalism (or better: Iconomy), Communism and Flowconomy).

	Ecological model		
Aspect	***Iconomy***	***Communism***	***Flowconomy***
Value orientation	Money	Should be: social	Happiness
Sharing of goods	Low	High	Middle
Change ability for people	Middle and decreasing[23]	Low	High
Focus on talent and sense	Low	Low	High

[23] People in Western countries *think* they are free. More and more they come to notice that they are trapped in the system. Systemjam. The Iconomy, the beast dictates their lives... and keeps them in an illusion...

	Ecological model		
Aspect	***Iconomy***	***Communism***	***Flowconomy***
Taking care of nature	Low	Low?	High
Way of collecting money for common purposes (eg. tax)	Hundreds of ways and rules, and increasing.	Don't know yet.	Three forms at maximum and far less than now.
Complexity of social structure	High (and increasing)	Middle	Low
Size of government paid staff	Enormous	Enormous	Small
Destructive debt economy	Yes	No	No
Plan economy	Partly	Yes	Only when necessary[24]
Type of money	Monopoly by the banking system+ black money	Monopoly by the government	Multicurrency, variety of local currencies, goodvalue exchange, no black money
Intrinsic inflation and un-proportional money creation	Yes	Yes, as far as known	No
Dominant format for economical organisations	Ltd (profit and possession orientation)	Na.	Flowcompany / foundation
Working orientation	Ego system / competition	Suppression / lethargy / working together	'We' systems / synergence / individual

24 A central guidance mechanism will only (try) to change the economy if it threatens inhabitants or nature in a unreasonable manner. If possible, there will only be local steering (by local communities).

	Ecological model		
Aspect	***Iconomy***	***Communism***	***Flowconomy***
			entrepreneurs
Innovation	High	middle	High
Efficiency	Low /middle	Low	High[25]
Copyright / patents	Yes	No / Na	Only when reasonable
Co-operation	Middle	Middle	High
Function implementation	Multiple	One time only	One time only[26]
Organic structure direction	Creation of hidden loss	Creation of hidden un employment	Creation of efficiency and sense[27].
Goods	Have, desire for more	Nave nothing / scarcity	Abundance, have little
Stress factor	Much	Much	Rest / freedom
Ethical change incentive	Bad conduct is rewarded / survival of the fittest	People locked in the system (not good)	Good conduct is rewarded / revival of the goodest
Creates sustainable products	No, Iconomy wants unsustainable things (more = more profit).	Average	High (no profit orientation, and single function implementation).

25 This might be one of the most surprising differences between the systems for the reader: see the Primary Iconomy constructors on the 'hidden loss gap' (why western economy has low efficiency). And the ideas on creating global associations (like Wikipedia, Linux development), via this perspective we see what a huge efficiency ump we can make. Each association takes care of a global function implementation; instead of many banks doing the same and competing, we have one association taking care of the (multi) currency system. Interesting note: within the anthroposophy creating associations was already mentioned hundred years ago, so these ideas are not new nor unique.

26 See footnote on efficiency.

27 People working at a certain organisation just leave the organisation if they feel they do useless work. Instead of creating work which happens in organisation and Iconomy system.

13.7 *Putting it to action*

13.7.1 The Flowcompany

I spoke in the chapter on the three Primary Primary Constructors (PIC) on the vehicles in which 'business' is done (or say it more nice: in which activity is concentrated). In the English world the 'Limited' with free floating stocks is widely used.

I also made clear that this type of vehicles are one of the roots of the misery the world is in now. Via accountability avoidance, focus on profit maximisation and possession accumulation.

If this vehicle brings misery, we need a replacement. I pose the name 'Flowcompany' for this. Martijn Brasem[28], a Dutch change maker and society designer, names the equivalent in his book 'Slave less enterprises'. He sees -correctly- the employer-employee relation as a form of modern slavery.

Main specifications of the Flowcompany:

1. It has no stocks. It is however allowed to collect money from people to co-invest, put there will be no such thing as profit sharing (in terms of money).
2. If the Flowcompany is terminated, its value is given to a good cause, society in general or another Flowcompany.
3. It may not take debt or put people in debt (as we know it).
4. All people working at the Flowcompany are in personal possession accountable for harm done to others. They can avoid this bye not taking liabilities or making promises.

[28] "Gelijkheid Vrijheid Verbondenheid", Publisher Deniesa. No English translation available (yet).

5. Trust is the basis.
6. The Flowcompany pays no tax[29]. This principle is based on the principle to reduce overhead in terms of administration and not to press the added value chain. This can change when the Flowcompany spoils the earth or acts not respectful.
7. There is no need to be enlisted in all kinds of government registers. Base idea is that these kind of registries merely are burden:the Internet has taken over its function.

The 'problem' with putting this to action is that it requires a change in legislation: the introduction of a new juridical entity. This can easily take up to five years, and it is expected that the 'institute' will block this concept as long as possible.

But.. the good news is that there is already a practical format which can be used: the foundation format. I think at least all Western countries know the foundation vehicle. So, for now, this vehicle is used as 'container of activity' in Novaglobe. See the section 'Flowconomy Maturity Model', further-on in this chapter for more ideas on this.

13.7.2 Practical solution for Greece, USA, etc.

Recently I decided to visit a Church ceremony. At a certain moment people started to speak the 'Holy Father' prayer.

Then my antenna's started to siren when I heard the words: "***And forgive us our debts as we forgive our debtors***".

Figure: The Holy Father:

[29] I will come back on the subject 'tax' in the Togetherhood chapter.

9 *Our father, which art in heaven: hallowed be thy name.*
10 *Thy kingdom come. Thy will be done on earth as it is in heaven.*
11 *Give us this day our daily bread.*
12 *And forgive us our debts, as we forgive our debtors.*
13 *And lead us not into temptation, but deliver us from evil. For thine*
is the kingdom and the power and the glory for ever and ever.

Wowwww....

What does this mean for our banks, as we want to head into the Kingdom come? Banks are *based* on *debt*. Nowadays banks cannot *survive* without putting people to debt. Banks cannot pass through Petrus' gate... sorry. We have to leave them at the entrance of Heaven...

So, can a good Christian actually work for a bank? I don't think so.

Putting people to debt is a sin, as I see it. A crime. At least when you take the goodvalue's, the Seven Principles of Reason, described earlier as a base.

Looking a little bit further in history I found this version of the Holy father:

Figure: An older version of the Holy father:

Our Father whyche art in
heauen, halowed be thy name.
Thy Kyngdome come.
Thy wyll be doen in yearth,
as it is in heauen.
Geue vs this daye our dayly
breade. And forgeue
vs our trespaces,
as wee forgeue them that
trespasse agaynst
vs. And leade vs not into
temptacion. But
deliuer vs from euill. Amen.

This version origins from 16th century [source: http://www.christusrex.org]

Why do I include this version? The word 'debt' has been replaced via 'det' (sounds like death, no?) to 'trespass'. So, trespass and (putting to) debt has a high resonance. Both are crimes.

Combine this with what we know about Islamic thinkings about debt (forbidden), and the feeling rises that even in pure Christian believing debt is no good. But that Western men have rewritten history in such a way that it is good. And when I talk with people about it they say: "No, no Iwanjka, that is only about the emotional side.". Will I think it is both material and non-material.

And no, mortgages are no good either. In my vision the 'mortgage' concept is a nasty trick of the Iconomy (the Beast) to make us taking huge debt, and using a wormtongue (see Lord of the Rings, Tolkien) style that it 'is no debt' because a house is given as repayment guarantee.

This is a lie.

High time to see through the mist of illusion (as the Maya's call it), or let is no longer be obscured by clouds (as Pink Floyd calls it). Let's face the ultimate truth.

And let's get rid of the banking system as we know it. Or put in a better way: do not implement it again in Novaglobe. More about the currency subject and how to do this in the new world.

Practical lesson

So, which practical lesson is in this for problems with Greece, USA, and... well which country not? The message couldn't be more simple: forgive the debts. All off them. And learn, and do not do it again...

I am afraid though, that our egocratic and complex system has become such a moloch with such an amount of bureaucracy, that it will proof impossible to get the spaghetti out of each other. The banking sector made a such maximum mix up of snipplets of loans and spreading it over hundreds of thousands of debtors... impossible to align all those persons in a plan. And than there is a kinds of juridical fuzz. Lawyers will jump on the 'breach' of contract cases like vultures. "And we will all go down together".

So, I am afraid, there is no other solution than let this whole system go bankrupt. And this will take quite some years... in the main time we should establish a fail over system, which can serve for a new ecology for the era to come...

And... if the Iconomy finds a way out of this: fine, than the two systems can co exist. But at least we have the security we do not depend on a fragile financial system anymore. It has no longer a monopoly.

13.7.3 Chivi currency: no inflation no debt

And then, one of the most important questions: "Is it possible to design a currency system which is more robust than the one we have nowadays?". The answer is: yes.

And it proofed to be a very simple system, which can be described at on page... Note: the Money chapter, earlier in this books describes the shortcomings and history of our current money system.

Chivi

Chi stands for good energy. Life energy. Vi stands for 'vitali' (alive) and 'go' (flow). Chivi is not money, it is a *type* of money. So, every one is free to implemented a chivi type of currency. I propose Greece introduces the Drachme again, next to the Euro (dual currency), based on Chivi. I propose the Netherlands to the same with the florin. I suggest each country does this, to shield itself from the coming financial turmoil when the debt balloon collapses.

Chivi derives from the abbreviation of "good value" (GV). Being good has a relation with the chivi around you... Chivi does not involve **interest**, **debt**, or un-proportional creation of the total amount of chivi in the system:

- The total amount of chivi in the system's 'body' is always 100.000 multiplied by the people participating in the system. '**Golden Chivi Checksum**'.
- When someone enters the community he/she gets 100.000 chivi by default. When he/she leaves, their balance will be set to zero and other balances will be adjusted in such a manner that the checksum applies again.
- The government establish a **maintaining foundation** which takes care of the required maintaining

functions for the chivi type currency. It is emphasised that the Chivi maintenance should <u>not</u> be outsourced to commercial banks. And that the ICT backbone should be kept ultimately simple... now we have the time to turn the pages over...

- Because there is no un-proportional money creation, there is no **intrinsic inflation** (like in our current money system) and thus no requirement to pay **interest** to the maintaining foundation.

Other practical remarks:

- Prices will settle by itself. Directly after introduction prices will fluctuate, but soon this will stabilise.
- It is preferred that all Chivi transactions are open for all (transparency goodvalue).
- A natura-exchange remains highly favorable... maybe one day we don't even need to use Chivi anymore...
- It is felt that It is better for now to introduce no physical money based on Chivi (practical issues). In the Netherlands we have a special card 'Chipknip' which can be used perfect to implement this dual currency system. Can be done in six months time. And via developing some apps on our handhelds, the money can float as easy as physical money.

13.7.4 Flowconomy Maturity Model (FMM)

As you have read in the 'Flowcompany' section: the most important thing, a vehicle to organise our 'activity' in already exists: the foundation. This vehicle is also ideal for storing possession. And granting guardianship to people from within the foundation. In such way you can live in a house, juridically owned by the foundation, for free... yes, this will be possible in the Flowconomy. Why not?

It seems wise to make a sort of 'grow' model for the Flowconomy. Take the CMM[30] (Capability Maturity Model) as an example: it has five levels, each level is defined by a set of criteria. 5 is the maximum level, 1 is the starting level. CMM and the Flowconomy are two totally different concepts, but as a an example of the idea it fits fine. Each higher level qualifies for the criteria of the lower levels.

Note that the Flowconomy on its own is an association as well.

Flowconomy Level criteria for <u>people</u>

FMM	Criteria
1	Not qualifying for one of the criteria below.
2	Has no debts or debtors (mortgage allowed). Monthly income max. 6000 euro (more is allowed if given away).
3	Lives modest. Gives money away to people who need it, instead of consuming it (via say luxury). Monthly income max. 5000 euro (more is allowed if given away).
4	Quantitative criteria: • Has no mortgage. • Works at foundation or is free entrepreneur. • Has no stocks in Limiteds or so. • Has no financial products (leverage plans, etc). • Has no personal belongings worth over 40.000 euro's.
5	Quantitative criteria: • Have no debt or debtors. • Income max 4500 euro monthly. • Possession worth max. 20.000 euro. • Gave goods (if any) to foundation (and gained guardianship possibly on them). • No retirement funds. • Works at FL4 foundation type or higher . Qualitative: Known as a giver, not a taker. Exchanges if possible in nature. Does not calculate 'prices' in euro.

30 Look on Capability Maturity Model, CMM in the Wikipedia.

Interesting to note that I am FL3... I am working to get rid of the possession of the two limits I own, I intend to transfer the stocks to a foundation or dismantle them. This process take some years, thanks to the present tax and accountancy rules... For the rest I am FL4 and almost even 5 (I hope / think).

Flowconomy Level Criteria for <u>foundations</u>:

FMM	Criteria
1	Not being one of the levels below.
2	[To be defined]
3	[To be defined]
4	Maximum salary (or paid to external staff): 4500 euro monthly. Average maximum salary: 2500 euro. Qualitative: Known as an non competitive, open organisation, open for synergy and cooperation.
5	[To be defined]

A design issue is whether it makes sense to defines 5 FL levels for the foundation (Flowcompany) as well. The criteria of leven five is left open, it might be a good idea to add criteria on eco-balance ans sustainability.

So, we need foundations to maintain our possessions. The Frhome type foundations are a nice example (see section below).

Why should people join?

I hear the reader say: "Yeahh, nice plans, but why should somebody want to join this thing?". My answer: because people's conscious will more and more tell this is the way to go. And it is reasonable. And you don't have to miss much luxury. Via living in such way I 'have' the luxury of a nice place where I can stay at Lanzarote. I was given the opportunity to stay a week in Athens at my previous Greek teacheres. All for free. If I had to 'buy' those homes where I stayed first... and than maintaining them...

And... withing the Flowconomy your level we be a bases for what is given from the association to you: jobs, guardianship on goods (amongst houses), etc. Via this we create that being good (defined as in the goodvalues) is rewarded. And than people will start to live automatically in this way. Because it brings them the key to a social network based on trust, abundance and safety. People in this network will be willing to share their goods and talents firstly to others in that same network and secondly to people residing in the Iconomy. Goodness united.

Putting the evolution of the **goodest** to action. And remember: if somebody is good, you will benefit from this goodness. This is the opposite of the survival of the **fittest** and somebody being better than you. You loose something is somebody is better...

13.7.5 Frhome – solution for housing and mortgage problem

As said earlier in this book: I see the mortgage problem as one of the biggest problems to be solved: in the Netherlands about 60% of the households has a mortgage. When people start loosing their jobs - in my eyes this is unavoidable due to economical dowturn- these people find themselves locked in their houses and eaten by the banks.

In the USA it common that you can turn in the keys of your house together with the mortgage. In the Netherlands it is not: you loose the keys and the house, but keep the -remaining of- the debt. And those debts will be huge due to dropping house prices. This can easily reach tons per family. The 'ordinary' will notice that they didn't read the little letters of the contracts they signed, or did not understood the consequences. Banks sales men tricked them into the thing, together with our politicians. Iconomy games.

You can imagine what this does with someone's feeling. The loose hope at once. Families break because of stress. Childrens childhood wasted. What kind of adults will they become?

So, I feel the only thing that will help is a **Mortgage-Pardon** plan. Relief the people from the mortgages. I want to found foundations of the Frhome type. Frhome stands for 'free homes'. The idea is to collect money via whatever way and than pay off the debt for the house, of a family in distress. The foundation becomes owner of the house.

The family than pays a yearly donation to the foundation of 1/30e of the debt amount the foundation paid for. After 30 years the house is free of the donations. And the family can live in it for free.

Why not?

Some other practical remarks:

- Via the foundation the 'guardian' of the house has the principal right on appointing the new inhabitants (probably often children or friends). Via this way we get rid of the fact that people need huge amounts of money to be able to live in a house.
- The guardian has considerable freedom in adjusting the house. This freedom is even enlarged when the house is 'donation free'. The idea is that a main reason for now to buy a house "That they can modify it" is fulfilled.

Remaining design issue:

1. What I don't know yet, if when somebody for instance creates an additional barn, whether this can be 'capitalised' (in money terms) when leaving... I feel this is not a good idea, because this will again give all kinds of pricing issues, and a new pricing rise

development. Somebody a good guideline for this issue?

Actually, I find the government should initiate a number of Frhome like foundations and do some initial funding. But when I look at the decisions politicians take in the Netherlands (only in the wrong direction), I am afraid , we -the people- must do it ourselves.

An alternative for people who get in financial problems is always just to go to the debt restructuring agency. Let the house being foreclosed. And enter the -at least- three year restructuring period or just go bankrupt[31]. I think this will be soon quite normal in the Netherlands to do. And I hope that people do it *before* they get psychic problems and enter the mental care domain... I have been there, but now time changed... more and more people see the reality of dropping house prices. Maybe we should create a foundation (agency) to help people with this process... but of course without asking money for this service, because money is the biggest fear for these people.

14 Eco subdomain III – Togetherhood

14.1 *Analysis*

First some observations on typical 'togetherhood' things. First let's take a look at a 'normal' life flow: You get born. You go to school. As from your teenagers years new concept enter your life: 'boyfriend' and 'girlfriend'. You get anxious and worried about getting the 'best partner available'. To me this process looks sometimes like a the 'rat race' which we see in business (careers). And both woman and man want to securitise the treasure the have conquered by marrying it, put a ring around each finger, sign a contract that we will be faith full to each other till eternity.

Why?

31

Is this logical?

I read somewhere that there are more than 1 million 'singles' in the Netherlands, and that this number is growing (on about 17 million inhabitants).

14.1.1 Marriage, singles and households

Why do we marry? Is it because in the 'earlier' days the man would leave his the woman as soon as he made her pregnant?

Is it because people cannot stand the feeling that in essence they are 'alone' on this earth? And need a feeling of control?

Is it something we do because everybody does it?

"Love is a bird", Madonna said that. And I believe her. Do not capture love.

And than, about one out of three marriages crashes and ends up in divorce. With so many, many practical issues, that many people just stay with each other only because of the practical 'shit' to be arranged: what about the children? What about the house? What about the mortgage?

And, here too, the system, the Iconomy swells on us marrying and locking us into one and another. A whole industry depends on it: divorcing advocates, notaries, etc.

Is the marriage (contract) sense full? Read this lyrics:

All I want is you [U2]

You say you want diamonds on a ring of gold
You say you want your story to remain untold.
*All the **promises** we **make***
From the cradle to the grave
When all I want is you.

You say you'll give me a highway with no-one on it
Treasure, just to look upon it
All the riches in the night.

You say you'll give me eyes in the moon of blindness
A river in a time of dryness
A harbor in the tempest.
All the ***promises*** *we* ***make****, from the cradle to the grave*
When all I need is you.

You say you want your love to work out right
To last with me through the night.

You say you want diamonds on a ring of gold
Your story to remain untold
Your love not to grow cold.
All the ***promises*** *we* ***break****, from the cradle to the grave*
When all I want is you.

Each time when I have to do my tax paying forms, and when I have to choose on my social status, I want to enter 'free'. Not 'single' or 'married', etc.

In the Netherlands more and more 'single' people arise...

The Iconomy says: "This is good for the housing market (more single mothers): all those single mothers need to buy a house...". Crazy system! This is really what I heard a housing market broker say... This seems in contrast to my earlier statement that Iconomy likes people as couples. But the Iconomy has created a smart rule for this: it is not allowed for groups of people to live together in a house (or at least we are gonna make this a cumbersome as possible). So it is for example very difficult for people, for example 'mothers with children' to live as a group. And thus even a mother without other people around her are forced to take a mortgage... at one moment she only working to pay the mortgage and the crèche, and does not see her children anymore. What kind of people will this give? (Adults / children).

Or more in general it is difficult to find a place for a group of people to live together as a group with all kinds of shared functionalities: sharing lowers GDP (gOvernment) and profit (Business).

And it seems everybody in the Netherlands has become happy with this 'separation' tendency, as I look towards the endless rows of houses and each garden fenced with a high and not penetrable wall or Hague.

> "The Iconomy strives to separate people maximally at the minimum space each."

And everyone wants more space, is not happy with only 10 by 10 meters of nature behind their house. And the only way to change this in our system is to get a higher salary, and to take a higher mortgage and buy more land.

Then I ask myself: why don't we share all those little peaces of ground with say 10 households? Than our children can run, we do not have to drive kilometers to drop of our greenery waste (we can arrange a little compost corner), we can go on holidays and our colleague citizens can cut the grass, etc.

Why don't we?

I think for the same reason we do not let our neighbors take care of our children: we don know, trust, like them, or have different ways of doing.

Than why don't we replace ourselves and find us a place with people which are more of our kinds? And make us a little livelihood?

Answer: because the system blocks us in each single step we want to take. In terms of finance: if you want to buy a different house in the Netherlands it costs you about 10%[32] of the prices, which on average comes down to say 30.000 euro's. Which takes about 3 years on average to earn. I call this a 'change penalty'. And once I started to look at society in such a manner, I saw change penalties everywhere.

And this it is not strange that even if we try to keep us free

32 Tax, notaries, bureaucracy.

from the spider glued lines, we sooner or later find ourselves as a brick in the wall. Especially when children enter our live.

And a last thing: why do you think so many 'fathers' are absent in their family? Or are totally 'consumed' in their career? Could it be they do not like the 'family' life in the same manner as woman do? But do not deer to say so, or maybe even more likely: cannot even feel that feeling? And of course each men is different, so do not generalise...

14.1.2 School

"We don need no education" sings Pink Flloyd. We -almost all- sing along an agree. But we do not take action. We do not response to this song? Sometimes I have the feeling that school is a nice place to put our children away. And the Iconomy does like that too, because than the parents can *work* and create GDP and pay for their debts and consume more. And the adults like it, because if they are free, can have a little time for themselves. Sometimes if have the feeling that schools are more like place to put children away, than a place which is good for them...

And probably all started good, or made sense. And some hundreds years ago people fought to make it possible for children to have education, and it brought welfare to many. So be respectful to the thing.

But times have changed. We have evolved. We have Internet. I have a friend in Athens, she is learning English almost completely by watching English movies. She likes it this way. I had three years French education at my school. I didn't like it, it was hard work for me, and I couldn't even have a conversation in France after that three years. Some years later, I became to adore France, became a rock climber and wanted to learn French. I think in one tenth of the time spent at school, I learned ten times more French. How? By translating French climbing magazine articles and putting the words I didn't now on my Iwanjka-specific word list, and rehearsing them. This was the way for me to do it. Intrinsic motivation is the key.

And why bringing our kids to music lessons, and all kinds of institutes, whilst we can teach them ourselves? We all have the required skills around in our friends group. Just activate them.

And maybe the most important thing: the skills required to be helpful and survive in this society changed completely. We do not have to stamp whole encyclopedia's in our head: they are with one click available on the web. *The web is the enabler of our combined wisdom and skills.*

So, we:

1. Do things far more efficiently than in the earlier days, because the required information, people and resources are far and far better accessible. Especially when make the move from the I-conomy towards the We-conomy (doing thinks together, sharing). The Iconomy (institutes) will protest, however. We can do with one day work, which our ancestors needed a week for.
2. Should focus on growing skills with our children which provide for this. Skills are: A. Finding out what the want and can add in this world (talent, sense), B. Communication, on the web, but certainly in physical form too, especially on emotional level, C. Organise their flow. Become organisers, all.

14.1.3 Crèches

Like many things, crèches have a good side and a bad side. First I want to start with the good side. As a father and observer of my daughters being at a crèche, I feel that being together with other young children is good. In this I believr.

But...

Crèches as we know them, for me are an ultimate expression of the Iconomy.

Crèches as we know them are an ultimate expression of the Iconomy.

Why?

Because the Iconomy has made us crazy. It said that it is necessary to have a career. Yeahh, it is good for the system, the Iconomy. Remember the 'coincidence' that a normal career path (and contract) is 30 years, the same time the bank needs you to pay off your mortgage (and more and more it seems we cannot pay this debt at all...).

And women really should develop themselves, and should not sit at home with children. The same goes for men actual. The bigger message: we all must work, full time!

And of course children are a problem then. We cannot put people to work with children. So we create crèches. Yeahh! And the good thing: they will make even more people go to work! For each mama or papa which enters the machine (work system), and starts to generate GDP, we also have about one additional worker at the crèche... so, two flies in one stroke! Those people start also to generate GDP.

And what is the result: the papas and mamas -who made a child to be with it in the first place- start to work. They have to pay huge bills to the crèche to take care of their kids. In the Netherlands it is not strange a complete income goes directly to the crèche. And who benefits? The Iconomy system... about say 70% goes directly as taxes towards the mouth of this system. So we feed the system with our children. Indirectly. Why are people taking care of our kids which have actually nothing to do with them? And Actually maybe about 90% of the money you earn for the crèche goes as tax into the system: One time tax when you earn the money at your employer (all taxes together could easily go towards 50%), and than you have to pay the crèche (say 19% sales tax on the bill), and the crèche company pays their employees leaving another 50% in taxes and so on.

With this example I want to make clear how endlessly stupid we are arranging things. And than I do not take in account the stress people experience to bring and get their children, the traffic congestion (in my place I think 30% of the cars kilometers in the morning in my city are caused by parents driving around with their kids). And of course the lack of a natural habitat: being with people which live around and with you normally. This gives quite some deprivation. Childhood ends. ADHD comes.

14.1.4 Overview main elements now and to be

Now	Togetherhood
Marriage or couple 'contracts'	Make it normal that people are free and individual people. They may have long term relations (of course), but do not institutionalise (church) or capitalise (banks - mortgages, tax agencies) them. Same rules and treatment for all. Let people based on their desires create relation formats which fulfill these desires. Freelations, poly amour, as long as respect is the basis, it is good.
Crèches	'Putting' our children together makes sense. But keep it in the habitat were they live normally. Arrange it with the people / families around. And keep money and government away. Arrange harmonies with all kinds of people: children, the elderly, the middle agers and the sick and 'weak'. Do not separate these groups.
School	No school 'law'. Education is a concern of the parents and / or the microhabitat where one lives in. Focus lies on other competencies than now.

14.2 Design – About an alternative

I do not say that people who want to remain in the 'existing' system should change. That is up to them. But I thing it is fair that people who want to live in another type of system can do so. So, society should introduce ways to choice for the alternative. Respecting the 'present' system as well. Make it dual boot, in software terms. You can switch on Windows, if you want so ('classical system', but you can also switch on Linux, and 'live in that world'). The latter is the Novaglobe system.

How to create this dual boot in a world which is more limitative than the one to be created, is interesting. Let's try. And regard the alternative per aspect.

14.2.1 Marry the Avalon way?

I once was talking with a woman on Lanzarote. She worked in a art gallery and was selling shell made rings. I was wondering what the meaning could be of the sentence "all the leaves are brown' [California dreaming song, The Mama's and Papa's]. And were the word 'marriage' came from', which for me felt like 'Mary's Age'. And I was wondering on my own 'broken' relation, which had held for 12 years. I never say 'ex- wive'. For me relations are not black and white. Why is the one moment somebody your dearest friend, and as soon as it is not any more possible to be an 'man and woman' you became enemies, and so much you liked to do with each other cannot be done anymore...

She said (the woman at Lanzarote): "Iwanjka, let me tell you about the Marry-ing ritual at Avalon: "In Avalon the man and woman give each other a ring *to set each other free"*. Hmmmm... that sounds quite different than we do it nowadays in 'western society'.

> "In Avalon, the man and woman give each other a ring to set each other free"

And I do not make thus up myself.

Could it be that the whole ritual about promising and has been made up by the church institute? Could be, it benefits from people who get locked in a certain situation. Feel unhappy after some years, and can say that they do not fulfill gods will and are guilty and are sinner. And via that way can keep control over them?

"The preacher man likes the cold, he wants me to stay" [Californian dreaming, Mamas and the Papas]

And 'all the leaves are brown', in the same song, could it be the people which stayed together longer with each other than was good for them? And then turned bittered and pale? Look around you in the city, how many happy couples do you see?

14.2.2 About the word 'California'

Back in the Netherlands, I was wondering about the word 'California', which came to me in so many songs. Sarra, my Greek teacheres learned me that 'Cali' means 'good'. Later, doing a project at the Dutch government a project member (Bhun) learned me that 'to fornicate' is an existing English word. I looked it up in the Wikipedia... this word had the biggest surprise in it of all the words which reveled themselves too me. To fornicate means: "Voluntary intercourse *before* the marriage". So California means:

California means "Good voluntary intercourse *before* the marriage"

For me this gave the missing key to some ultimate truth. Songs for me often hold an tremendous deeper meaning. Listen to Californication song of the Red Hot Chili Peppers, listen to 'Californian Dreaming'. Listen to the good vibrations sounds of the beach boys (which for me has a huge California surfing association). And so many other expressions with California in it. I believe that names and words are resonator points. They *are* sound. We consist of sound (like quantum physics make clear). So, it could be very well possible that all kind of knowledge is encrypted in words, how impossible it may seem.

Well, whatever you feel with this, do with it what you want.

For me it makes clear that a thing I logically already derived from my own observations (how many couples in a pizzeria look happy with each other? I counted one out of five?): marrying and promising love is as letting your anchor down. In Californian terms, when the love was good and voluntary before the marriage, what does it do once the marriage is a fact?

And why do something which might cause negative things, which is not really needed?

Of course, there are people which feel free as a bird in their marriage. Which, when they wake up the morning think: if I had the totally free choice, I would prefer to be with the partner which lies besides me (or without somebody in the bed at all). But many are not.

14.2.3 Iconomy made derivatives on your marriage promise

And the worse is that the 'system' has made 'derivatives' on the marriage: banks have based the amount the lent to you on your marriage-promise. The government builds all kinds of constructions around your marriage. When you feel like undoing it, you are far deeper in trouble than in the case you only would say: "sorry, I break my promise, bye...". That is the most evil part.

And the last thing which I want to say about the marriage, then I'll stop: the people marrying you in church, the priests, they should comply to the words of Mozes: "do not lie". But what they do is to make 1/3 of the people say a lie directly under their nose. Is that good? I do not think so... They know, because one out of three divorces...

Intention to be long with each other is enough I would say. But banks do not like intentions. You cannot take a mortgage on intention. So, this the way it is all connected.

For me high time to add a Novaglobe way of marrying, and do it the Avalon way, or at least let it be a celebration of love, direction and situation, and make no promises, only intentions...

For me a primary -practical- reason to promise to stay with each other is that is to safeguard a period of say 20 years to grow the children. So, this is an important part to arrange for in the togetherhood.

14.2.4 Microhabitats

For me the most logical way I want to live is a thing I started to call 'microhabitats'. "Ah, a commune", I hear many say. Maybe yes, maybe no. I do not know how a 'commune' has been defined. I did some research on how the many 'communes' which were created in the '70s and '80s did vanish. My mother almost became a San Yasin (A Bhagwan follower).

I think they broke (many) because of the fact that it became obligations. And that within these communities people took charge which were not the most 'balanced' people, not the most talented for this job, and probably got way to manifest themselves in this world. The same happens in many foundations I see (and other organisations): no organic renewal, no ongoing flow is at hand in the organisers 'tree', and than sooner or later, the tree will loose it leaves (the people of the community). And I think they also broke down because of jealousy and 'couples' forming... (even there).

I will not go in depth into the microhabitat constitution, I thin it could take a whole book on 'construction' principles, and best practices, and I do not think there is one 'fit'. I only fee that these microhabitats form the basis for our way forward. Some key elements are:

- A free flow of the members, resulting in maximizing the chance that people with the same 'tuning' will live together. A free flow directly means that when there is a mode of buying a part when one comes, and selling a part when one leaves, will not work. In other words: try to keep (big) money away,.
- A guardian should be in charge. And some kind of model

should be at place to provide for organic renewal, and tuning of the 'groups' policy with its members. I think the Harminocracy model can arrange for this.

- People probably want to have their own private rooms. The group decides on which shared functionalities will be build (eg. a shared canteen, fitness room, etc).
- Do not uniform the microhabits: people who have common interests just flock together and create their thing. So all kinds of habitats and 'mini infrastructures' can arrange. That is why we should make all kind of 'building' legislation fade: it only allows for more bricks in the wall type of houses....

Some other things I believe in:

- To have elderly and children live together in a Microhabitat. This provides for the functions in society which are now capitalised by the Iconomy: crèche and elderly institutes. Both making all people feel more and more deprived. And... I think we cannot give the care to these people via the iconomic way (separate people and arrange paid staff to take care).
- That it should be not be necessary to move around with young children for more than 500 meter frequently (daily, school, crèche, etc). This requirement is fulfilled automatically with the Microhabitats. And keep the money out of taking care for for children!
- That we should forget about classical thinkings on education. Make it free for parents to raise there children as they want it. And let them be the teachers of the children the way they want it. And let the people living in the Microhabitat be teachers as well... Stop meddling with this (government staff can advice and notice when things seem to go out of hand, that remains a good thing).

Consequences are:

- That -in the Netherlands- the construction laws should be adjusted. At this moment it is for example not allowed to make a house suited for more people due to size restrictions: I wanted to live at my mothers house, with plenty of space to enlarge it. This was not allowed. Instead the system 'forced' me to take a mortgage (of course) and buy a place of my own. Which was far too big for me to maintain, together with a child and paying for a mortgage. Why wasn't I allowed to live with my mother? An example of the 'Iconomy separation syndrome' at work.
- That house prices will drop, due to the fact that the pressure on the housing market is relieved. Good for the people, but the Iconomy does not like this. Remember the banks which drive almost completely on mortgages and remember the government which is in the 'complot' (unconsciously) which pays their employees buy keeping ground prices extremely high and selling things which originally belong to the people to the people. And the Iconomy has made most people accessory or stakeholder: more than the half of the people have paid enormous amounts for their houses and are not willing to see prices drop. See again a typical Iconomy driven loop leading to the fact that something what is good for the people cannot be done. Therefore, I believe, we need the mortgage-pardon plan, as depicted already in the Flowconomy chapter.

14.3 About government and 'taxes'

In the Flowconomy chapter I mentioned I would say things on 'government' and 'taxes' int the Togetherhood section. I decided to position this subject within this eco subdomain because government is about 'things we want to arrange together'. And government is coupled to 'tax' (and how to raise it).

Firstly I believe in a direction in which people instead of doing work X, make money, pay tax and let others do work Y, we can do that work Y more ourselves. Taking care of our children ourselves (instead of crèches which are paid for the half by the government).

And instead of having all kinds of city cleaning companies driving around, we can take care of cleaning our parts ourselves. Or better: do not let them pollute.

14.3.1 Who is the government?

A next thing is: what should the government do? But first... what *is* the government? Is it all those people on the payroll of a thing called 'government'? I prefer to see it as 'all those people who get there salary direct or indirectly the tax profits'. In the Netherlands yearly tax profits is about 130 billion euro's.

Looking at it via this way I notice that maybe around half of all the people working in my country can be considered to be directly or indirectly government staff (via this definition I also account the craftsman who builds a new government office, or is making a new highway).

Hmmmm, that could be another hidden loss gap, no? Because the other half has to work harder and harder, longer and longer to provide for the necessary essence (which is money these days, in terms of tax).

So my first observation is that within Novaglobe the amount of people paid by tax income should be far, far less. Maybe at most 10% of the total working force or even less. If we can arrange that things are done more and more by local communities or local communities provide for required skills and value in natura (man hours, goods, etc), this shouldn't be a problem.

Government model should have an incentive to remain lean

and mean, or even -looking at the huge thing now- should get leaner and leaner

I already explained in the part on analysis why the government grows bigger and bigger (GDPBeast), let us not make that fault again... In terms of the Misery Creation Syndromes: the Fattening Syndrome at work (see appendix).

The interesting point on politics: the first political party proposing this would be decimated, already because the major part of the people are working *within* the government. So the government, the system did a great thing: it made enough people dependent on it to ensure that it can grow on and on. But like a cancer growing in its host, it will kill its host, and thus itself.

14.3.2 On tax and costs of the government

And I believe in a direction were we simplify our economy and rule system (including the government), and apply ICT is a sense full manner (not as now building computer systems over and next to each other), we can reduce costs for our government easily without 50% And I even believe with 15 years with 90%.

So, imagine that you have to pay say 70% less tax, than the whole discussion on who has to pay tax and via which manners become less relevant. And I think we should end up with maximum three manners of paying tax, and maybe some sort of fixed tax: everybody pays yearly as same amount. No complex administration processes anymore, balance sheet calculations, etc. In the book 'New Netherland[33]', by Dutch Economist Jan Frank Koers, he points out a practical plan on this topic too. And we should get rid of the difference between 'black' and 'white' money. Which can be done easily by making things more simple.

[33] This book is unfortunately only available in Dutch. Publisher: Elikser.

14.3.3 Base income for all?

An idea which is fundamental in the party program of the political party New Netherland is to give everybody a base income of say 1000 euro's a month. The money is available when we stop with the mortgage stimulation tax reduction program, and remove nearly all kinds of specific welfare payments (and replace them with the base income). The latest gives work for thousands of government staff. An evil thing is that these regulations keep people caged in their social security instead of getting stimulated to start doing useful things in society. This measure will give a tremendous simplification of our system.

So I find it in its base a very good plan: it makes people free to quite with jobs they don't like, change positions, etc.

But... it is based on money. And I see - I am sorry to say that - so much people (via the buddywork I am doing) who just cannot deal with money: they spent they money at drugs, luxury, whatever, but not to pay the rent of their apartment. And thus end up in problems, and costing society about triple the welfare payment they get initially.

And it keeps us tied to the 'Iconomy' (because we use Iconomy-money). I would propose the following:

Don't give money, but arrange for the underlying intended 'base-facilities': a home, food, security, care, public transportation, school. For free. Make them guardians of a place. And give about 50 euro's a month at maximum as 'luxury' money.

People can make more money if they want more luxury, want to drive a car....

This solution direction is related to the 'how to make people free for the world shift' section in Part III of this book as well...

So you see a sort of two levels coming: 'base-facility' to live, and on top of it a luxury level. The base-faculity forms the basis of the Maslow Pyramid, and if we abandon a debt based Iconomy, people will stay in the top, and don't rocket through the good spot and end up in the base of the Flipped Maslow.

14.3.4 On localities

I think it is wise, as said already in the Harmonicrazy chapter to strive for more cohesive localities: people knowing each other, coming to each other, doing things together for their livelihood. The Iconomy now prevents this (via mortgages, high rent, shortage of houses, legislation, etc.). I see the following locality sizes:

- Microhabitat: A living habitat up to 50 people implementing the opposite of microseperation and implementing a senseless place for children to be. Eldery, young, middle agers and people with a 'deficit' living together. Don't huzzle around daily with children towards a crèche and even maybe not to a school (do schooling at the habitat).
- Minihabitat: The same as microhabitat but at village / city area level, Say up to 2500 people. Organised via harmoicracy principles.
- Mesohabitat: The same as minihabitat but at city level , say up to 120.000 people.
- Macrohabitat: The same as mesohabitat but at metropole level, say up to 6 million people.
- Omnihabitat: The same as mesohabitat but than for the world (all above mentioned habitats are represented via the omnihabitat harmoncracy at world level).

Via this way things organise and evolute in an organical

manner.

14.3.5 Plan and execute cycle of each locality

What I believe in is a fairly simple governments plan-and-do cycle:

- Organise a continuous, rationalised process on plan making on all kinds or issues, at all kinds of levels.
- Take a snapshot once a year.
- Make a year plan based on that input, adjust seven year plan.
- Execute the plan.
- Simple as that.

This is - of course- related to the Harmonicracy subdomain.

As stated earlier ICT is the ideal instrument to get the input from the people to the steering team. But this should be accompanied by regularity mini seminars in eg each big city, were people talk and discuss topics. Topics are elaborated in more depth in between seminars, results are presented before the next round and thus, in a controlled and rationalised way everybody has a voice, can post his or her idea at the appropriate level, and gets an answer, which is a responsibility of the hooder to take care of.

14.4 What should all people do, which come free?

The closer reader will have noticed that in all kinds of branches we can do the same thing (or said better: the reasonable part) with far less people. What should all those people who come free do? And how should the earn their money?

The answer on the last question is that theoretically the

added value to the society is still being created, but by far less persons. So, in theory, their even should be enough money to pay the people who came free.

Those people can do more sense full things. Work enough. And if we / they decide they don't have to work (which I think is a good thing, that we work less), let them do what the find useful... let them inspire themselves...

14.5 A practical proposal for 'immigrant problem'

Martijn Brasem proposes in his book (see the appendix on books) a solution that each 'well developed' country adopts a 'poor country'. And thus a far more focused support line is being created. And it creates more involvement, etc.

I see a interesting opportunity with the 'immigrant' problem: at a certain moment it seems fair that a certain country states it cannot adsorb more people from foreign countries and cultures without getting dis-balanced itself.

I want to participate in the creation of new townships in for example Africa (where a lot of space seems to remain). And within those townships I propose to create a 'shifted' ecology, right from the beginning: eco-balance with nature, a safe township where you can leave your door open, people living in much more harmony, etc.

And we do this with intelligent application of new technology like the Internet, making illegal behaviour transparent (and avoiding criminals to enter the township), intelligent application of resource balancing, solar panels for energy, etc.

And we do this in co-operation with local people: the 'western' country brings in skills and probably materials. In return 'western' people can come to stay there in wintertime (or longer). An advantage for local people can be that things like schools, health care, agriculture become available directly for people living around it for say a distance of 50km. We keep the money and profit-oriented companies out. Only flowconomy style is allowed.

Now the 'immigrants' come in. Imagine that we -for example in the Netherlands- offer this people a three year stay, rest, education. A good life. In return people intend to go further to one of those new townships. Which more and more become like oasis in a stress full and intoxicated western society. Places where people *want* to live.

Discussing this with my room mate Don Willard, he says: "Why should 'immigrants' go to the Netherlands first at all? I wouldn't be surprised those people want to go to those new townships directly". I think he is right.

A nice example (to me) of the resource based economy RBE, see the Zeitgeist movie), in which we share our world in a far more sense full manner.

And.. a last important remark: the *goodness* of the regime in the country on which we will focus is crucial. Bandit-style regimes who now are un-reliable, plunder their own people, etc. will be excluded from participation. Until they proof to be 'good enough'. These countries will see neighbor countries flourish and will ask themselves: why is that? The answer is: "Better be good". And thus goodness will be rewarded. And if that country remains 'evil' for their people, the people simply might migrate to a place which is better for them. And the 'peaceful' country will feel its back secured by its supporting country...

I think this could work. Why not?

14.6 Summary

Various topics were discussed in this chapter. I think the most important one is that we start to examine the microhabitat as a normal living place. Where we know see one or two adult-person households as the base of our society, let's add a concept of say 5 to 15 adult-person households. And see how this works.

Via this way a kinds of 'things' which are now arranged with money can be done in a more humane way: taking care of our children, schooling, taking care of our elderly taking care of the sick. And besides this it makes that we have far less traffic movements, have to earn less money, and have more time for our primary relation to do things with (you don't have to arrange a babysitter each time, there is a 'pozzy' around). And maybe we have time to grow our own vegetables and fruit. Have our own micro eco places, with solar panels included.

The last section was about 'government'. Actually the government is about arranging things for our common benefit, I feel it has become far too big and takes over more and more functions which it does or inefficient, or which can be done by the people themselves. By organizing the government far more logically, and let all kinds of hidden loss gaps go, we don't need that much tax. And than the collection of tax isn't a big issue anymore as well. I see it as important to let go of the difference between black and white money.

15 Eco subdomain IV - Humansound

"What is the sound of a sound human?"

Sound has intuitive equivalences in various languages: Sound, sense, zin, zon, zijn.

This subdomain is about healthy people. How to *avoid* getting them unhealthy, and about how to repair, or maybe better re balance there state once dis balanced.

I feel it is good to put a broad range together:

- Physical balance, nowadays called 'medicine'
- Mental balance, nowadays called 'mental care'

Some words on physical well being

The scope of this chapter is both physical wellbeing and mental wellbeing (or maybe better: *emotional* wellbeing). On the subject of physical well being I don't have that much to say, that It would justify several pages (and want to keep this book within 250 pages). I think as a 'science' medicines do a good job. I have only to say this about it:

1. I think too often emotional-practical causes are not taken in account in the diagnoses (imagine somebody having pain in the back frequently). And thus no real solution is organised, this probably has to do with, the second point. And too often a patient gets loads of pills to swallow (blood, chemicals, heart, etc.).
2. I think that the Iconomy has a far too big role in medicine. A medicine has only 10 or 20 minutes per consult in the Netherlands. Insane, I feel. And It should not be allowed for iconomic pharmaceutical parties to visit medicines with 'information', 'training' and their products.
3. Too less is done at prevention: a doctor would not get a income if there where no sick people. This 'Iconomy' thing we should be removed in the new world. A doctor should use his talents in such way to strive for no patients at all. And we should strive for prevention: people living emotionally balanced and physically balanced (sports???).

A final not on the physical aspect:

Physical wellbeing: our care systems become more and more equipped to repair all kinds of malfunctions. Maybe even too much. I heard a professor stating that the Darwinistic physical evolution had came to end because of this. A main cause of death, cancer, we still cannot be cured. More and more voices I hear, that cancer maybe a consequence of stress, too less physical exercise and too much meat / bad food. Maybe instead of repairing things, we should more focus on prevention.

I continue on the mental care system side.

15.1 Analysis

Observations:

- Take a look at the numbers on antidepressants : about one out of 10 adults in the Netherlands takes them. And the Netherlands being one of the most peace full, civilised and liberal countries on earth.
- It feels like more and more people are drifting around. This is logical: all kinds of old predefined paths vanish. All kind of local traditions vanish because Internet and globalisation came. We all need a new kind of religion. Maybe we can create one: "Sense & Reason"? Psychiatry and pharmacy took us into a misleading path. Down the hill. Creating 'mental sicknesses' and pills for pretty logical things. Read my other book 'Lifejam diagnosis' if you are interested in an in depth research and case rationale on this topic. This was -of course- driven by the Beast. By Iconomy. Not wanting to get unveiled.
- The DSM V (the psychiatric bible) will proof itself that psychiatric theories on diseases need to be fundamentally redefined. This 'science' got itself into a swamp. See the serpent eat its tail. If you

wish, read my book 'Diagnosis Lifejam[34]' on why psychiatry went of the proper path so far, and for a proposal in redesigning the basis.

15.2 Requiremtents / prerequisites

1. Viewing point of the human 'being'. See a human as a collection of his physical, rational, emotional and soul body. And see the essence as energy and vibration and not material. I find a combination of scientific findings, especially in quantum physics, at the one hand, and a more spiritual way, as we can find in Buddhism as a proper way to move fore ward.
2. Focus on *prevention* of people getting 'ill'.
3. Keep the big money out.
4. Back to nature and reason. A recent decision by the EU to ban nature based medicines is a step in the wrong direction.
5. Connect with sense and vocale (and thus things like religion / spirituality, sensegiving).

A note on the word 'ill' or 'disease'. The wikipedia state that there is no clear definition for this word, so we should be careful when we use it.

15.3 Design

The main focus will be laid on the 'mental' side of our wellbeing (and which, I wouldn't be suprised could cause about 50% of our physica malfunctions).

15.3.1 Prevention

It all starts with a sound society. Release tension. Release stress.

[34] See appendix on related books.

Prevention Children

While writing this section I sit in the train from Bruxels towards Amsterdam. I get distracted frequently by the penetrating sound of two little children next to me. Boy I guess 4 years old, girl I think 3. Mother is telephoning. Man is sitting silent with them, I guess it is the father. Mother is giving boy frequently annoyed gestures to stop something. Girl is constantly manifesting herself. Jumping in between woman and boy. Asking endlessly for food. Talking. Picking at mothers hair. This goes on and on.

"The mother must get crazy...", I think. And to be honest, I start wondering once again why people want children at all.

And, more, why we do it in this way, with all pression coming down too much on a few.

Having children is heavy. I know that now, as a father. I feel it is not 'something just to do next to it'. And because so many people have children, combined with their own compressed schedules, children become disharmonic. And psychiatrists, always finding a disease, start putting pills in them. And often it has to do with the setting of the children, and maybe the parents. As I think was the case in this example: the parents seemed totally unhappy with each other, the situation, whatever...

I think we should give the way we treat and raise our children a fundamental twist. And, as I state in the 'togeterhood' section, for people open to it, sharing of children could be a key into a more sound future.

And...sick children now will give sick and dis balanced adults later.

15.3.2 Prevention – Adults

I will put less words on this one. Just read the chapters on

Flowconomy and Togetherhood. And the 'Wind of Change' section, on stress, pressure, etc.

I believe when we create the proposed society, at least 70% of the people will have less mental 'problems' and physical malfunctions. But, again, our present health care (industry) does not want that. They loose 70% of their clients, and 70% of their profits. Therefore, again: the fundamental 'underground' in our new ecology should be that people are happy to <u>not</u> being needed anymore as a health care employee.

15.4 Restoration

I believe in a world in which more and more people start to cure each other, instead of consulting all kinds of therapists. And I think we can reduce pills consumption with at least 90%.

In the Netherlands we put his kind of 'buddywork' already to action with a network of engaged people (voluntary). And to my opinion: with success.

I believe the psychiatric sickness model is based on misinterpretations and all kind of created sickness labels. It has lost track a long time ago.

In the 'Diagnosis Lifejam book, a profound proposal for a complete redesign of the mental system', I state that the majority of all sickness labels probably have the same cause categories, which are:

1. Emotional trauma (like abuse in youth or lack of affection as child), and / or,
2. Practical causes (like having debts, problem in work, locked in relations), and / or,
3. Suffering form bad elements in our society (like Veronica decides to die, in the book of Paulo Coelho).

And bringing it back to this essence it becomes clear the majority of our mental care system and psychiatry looses its basis. Ike DMS IV, this book can be send to the paper shredder right away. But more important and positive: new, far simple and efficient ways of treating people emerge. Because we finally focus on the real problems of patients, and not on the labels made up by a being out control science-industrial complex: the present psychiatric-farmaceutical complex.

A new (mental) care system will be based on:

- Social helpers and reorganisers. A company in distress we organise, so should we -often- do with peoples lives, or at least help them reorganizing.
- Buddy contact. Organise contact with people who have gone similar situations and feelings. There is practical evidence that this works. This not the case with nearly all psychiatric treatments.
- See for a full example of an alternative the RdRemedy approach as described in Diagnosis Lifejam.
- Rehome places: small scale places where people can go and live. To make a transition. At this moment people can only end up in psychiatric hospital when they cannot manage their life anymore (and more and more people will break down due to economical crisis and social deprivation).

16 Eco subdomain V - Artscience

This chapter is about the domain embracing arts *and* science.

16.1 Analysis

Looking around I notice some things:

- Art has become an icon. People talk about art. Rich people pay enormous amounts of money for 'true art'. So, art has become capitalised. Like love did become capitalised (prostitution).
- Less and less people seem to have time for expression themselves. How many people dear to sing? And how often the environment makes them to stop. People feeling themselves not good enough, to express themselves.
- In music we have or big pop stars, or the audience. We make idols out of musicians. This killed Michael Jackson, I believe. This killed Kurt Cobain, I believe. They died under the pressure of the Beast, the Iconomy. Mozes doesn't say without a reason: do not make an idol! What do we watch on television? Idols. How much bigger should be the writing on the wall. One of the reasons television has left my life.
- Sports has become spoiled by destructive competition, drugs and big money. And again idols, icons. Iconomy at full speed. Tour the France? All about drugs. Football? All about hooligans fighting. Even the holy Olympic games do not feel to be about global brotherhood and physical enlightenment.
- Science is becoming more and more commercialised. In the Netherlands there are, for example, no

scientific conferences anymore on mental care which are not funded my the pharmaceutic industry.

- Science more and more have to work on a commercial basis, which makes it more inefficient and dull: like trying to get as much references as possible in published articles. And where the big money enters, so enters the focus on things which cost money (for the consumer), or gain profits for companies. So everything is getting more and more expensive, and free available simple solutions are being pushed out. The wrong way around.
- My last example is about a student artist I happen to know. He quite his study for the third time. It makes him feel depressed, the institute. We talked about it. Over-rationalised art I call it. What happens? The institutes are like trees, beginning little. They grow. The people who flourish there are the ones who did not manage to become true artists themselves (I exaggerate a bit). Or, are being pushed by Iconomy are forced to rationalise art. They write thick books about it. Create models. And the most painful: they define criteria one 'good' and 'bad' art. Art is expression, coming from the heart and earth. When somebody, especially somebody sensitive expresses himself, and get criticised, that is is 'not good', it is as saying: your feelings are bad. Stop it. Not possible, and killing the spirit.

16.2 Requirements

This is interesting. And dangerous, put 'requirements' (which are pretty rationale things) on a non rational thing like art. But I think we can state some sense full remarks here:

- Take the **pressure** out. Inspiration and pressure is

like combining water and fire. Ask a painter to make his most beautiful painting in before 12h clock next day. It will not work.

- Take **destructive competition** out. But then, there is a fragile stage in which motivation and competition are related. Therefore I say *destructive* competition. Maybe it is enough to take the big money out of it...

- Provide for **organisational renewal**: make sure people working at science or educational institutions do not work there for ever. And even put a end of life to institutions: create new institutions, and let the others fade (with respect). Seems like a wast of capital, it is not.

- Implement **global constructions** right from the bottom. Which cooperate. A global school of mathematics, a global school on emotions, a global school on art, etc. Of course local colors should be given a maximum of space.

- Implement a **global wikipedia**, definitions only once declared, and than translated to various languages. This will improve global cooperation and understanding, and it will release millions of man hours for in depth study and description (hours now used to align definition over all those languages and to make descriptions per language). Local and cultural descriptions are added on top of the global descriptions.

16.3 Design

How to put this in action?

The nicest thing would be when all people who want to do something in science or arts could rely on a base income. I addressed this topic already in the Togetherhood section. Or basic facilities, like food, a roof, care, etc.

In the Netherlands the government is doing the opposite: it is eliminating a special payment for artists. I believe the good thing about it is that all kinds of rules and control systems -hopefully- vanish too. Like government staff chasing artists and controlling their production.

The bad thing about it all is that some artists will be forced to survive by doing typical commercial work like making endless series of fountain statues (I once worked some weeks for an artist doing this, he hated it, so that is why I was hired, he preferred to make unique statues, but couldn't live from it).

Experimental work or 'too hours-intensive work' will die, because it can not be commercialised of capitalised by the Iconomy.

I actually see only one real solution: implement the Flowconomy. Implement thus the ideas behind the Venus project. Thus all people will only have to work say one or two days a week instead of six. And thus a lot of time remains for those who want to create 'arts'.

These arts will be created without stress. So true expression and love will be put into these artifacts. And these artifacts will only have to cost the price of the materials which were put in it.

And than, finally, all those arts can flow to the people enjoying it. And thus Veus and Earth (art) might meet again...

Amen.

17 Eco subdomain VI - Justitea

Well let's take a look at our justice system, including the part which takes care of law and order (police).

> *"Then came the churches then came the schools*
> *Then came the lawyers then came the rules"*
> [Telegraph Road, Dire Straits]

Need I say more?

17.1 Analysis

What should justice take care for?

Justice should make sure that people who do wrong get an appropriate sentence. Police should take care for law and order. Both should work in an efficient manner

Numerous are the headings in our news papers on criminals who are released because of a procedure fault. Numerous are the stories where the victim gets punished instead of the offender. And a last headline I right was that the Dutch police could hardly solve any robberies and crimes.

Looking at the core elements of the system it is not strange that this happens: the systems benefits from more clients (people being robbed, etc.), that offenders do it again (and become 'clients' again), and that there is little to no attention in *avoiding* crimes (because than they wouldn't have clients anymore).

And of course the money thing has ruined the whole function dramatically: lawyers costing victims 300 euro's an hour. Completely insane... yeahh you can get a pro deo lawyer... but which lawyers wants to work like this?

And than the Iconomy beast jumps in even more: insurance agencies selling 'juridical assistance' assurances. And when I want to do my work as an consultant I have to take such an assurance. All hidden lost gap examples.

A lawyer without bandits has now income. So, what kind of world those this system create? Right a world with bandits. And I have the feeling criminals often have money, and they victims don't. So guess who wins the lawsuit?

As a salesman you often have to lie. In the Netherlands it is accepted that brokers on houses lie. I think lawyers often lie or don't speak the whole (relevant) truth as well... with as argument that they need to protect the privacy of their client...

Example: Laws on drugs

Today, I signed a petition for regulation on hard and soft drugs in the Netherlands. The organizing foundation 'Drugs policy', states that the present policy in the Netherlands 'forbidding drugs' is accountably for at least the half of the criminality. They propose to make the drugs legal, and apply sound procedures and quality control on giving them to people. About 800.000 of the 17 million people living in the Netherlands take drugs. They are available everywhere, but still are illegal. Strange, no?

"Hey?", I think: "So, they (the juridical institute) made a law which brings them a lot their clients?" (making drugs illegal). "And now the same people should decide to make that law go?"... It is all about money. As long as we do not fundamentally change the system these kind of nonsense making laws will remain.

Example: Law over Value, Dutch politicians are allowed to lie

And one of the most tear pulling examples: after the latest Dutch elections, some politicians in the parliament proofed to have lied about their past (and thus hiding important 'criminal like' facts, which if they were known would have blocked their way to the parliament). They where allowed to remain in the parliament...

A system which is so sick that this can happen should be replaced immediately no? Lying is a base ground value which is wrong, and which should have appropriate consequences....

One of my favorites credos now:

> I rather be an outlaw and invalue, than inlaw and **outvalue**. The Dutch justice and political system is the second... (in law, but out value, not living the virtues).

So, let's try to reformulate the requirement for our new justice system:

Requirements

The Justitea system is there to:

1. Bring justice when somebody feels offended. The basis for this are the common values like not lying, stealing, etc. Rules and laws are secondary. 'Because these are the rules' we don't want to hear anymore. Reason goes over rules (or change the rules when not reasonable, or make them 'guidelines').
2. *Prevent* that people become criminals, have bad conduct. Especially at schools attention should be given to this topic. Possession, and people in distress and / or taking drugs probably have above modal chance to slip into bad conduct. So a close working relation with the Togetherhood eco subdomain is required.
3. Do this in a as simple and efficient possible manner. As long as due to complex rule systems base values

(see chapter on the goodvalues) are trespassed the system should be simplified. The 'money density' of all people working in the system should be far less, because otherwise greed takes over justice...

17.2 Design

Looking at the requirements, and the system with many, many rules and laws we have nowadays, and the knowing that renewal is a logical step in our evolution, let's start from scratch.

And this time we try not to end up into the 'lawyers and rules' thing we have nowadays. We have learned.

And do we actually need rules? Or can we live with guidelines as well? The problem with rules, is that they become more and more complex, end each time more and more detailed, and that people applying them do not take notice of the idea behind the rule anymore. Or, and that is often the case, cannot do that because somebody else will say they have trespassed a rule. Rules makes that there is no more room for reason, sense and thinking. Rules will make fools...

> I know a festival where 250 people live together for four days without rules... there are hooders though. And shared values. Good we go on for 10 days? 100? 365 days?

Let's at least try it with a minimal on rules. Maybe it is good to call a velocity constraint for cars a rule. Like '50km an hour maximum'. When we would make this a guideline, we can suspect long talks with somebody driving 60km an hour and saying it was not dangerous. But the special thing is, that what this man or woman says could make sense. And makes us think about the 'requirement' behind the rule. So, maybe at least, each rule should have a requirement and a clear owner within the harmonicracy structure: who is accountable for the rule? I the Netherlands we have many, which I call 'Zombie rules'. I ask an government officer: "Why do we have this rule?", and I get an answer which I cannot logically understand, and I ask: who is thw owner of the rule, so I can talk with him / her? The officer looks at me why I ever, ever, can ask something so stupid... and that is the problem.

To few people ask 'stupid' questions. And so the rules can linger, grow, split and multiply. Systemjam, the beast is a fact.

In addition I would propose that more things are arranged *between* people direclty. Without fighting and lawyers. The first thing a lawyers says: "Deny!", and "Stop talking". How many divorcing people end up fighting in court by this? Then the two advocates jump into the arena (probably the best paid gladiators ever), and fight for the cause of 'justice'. Leaving the people who try to get thing thing solved in even a bigger mess than they were before, and financially pretty ripped.

In the Netherlands you now are forced to go to a lawyer if you want to divorce and have children. Will cost you at least 1.500 euro's. Who do you think created this rule, or who advised it?

How can we arrange for that, that more things are taken care of between people? The vision I have is the one of an Indian clan. Where one inhabitant goes to the elderly leader, saying another inhabitant did do him wrong. The chief calls both people to his place and asks them both their story. If he feels it is needed, he takes a walk and ask people who where witness of things.

If he has enough information he comes with a 'judge' or

proposal. And, wise as he is, he first asks the offender how he thinks he could made up with the victim (settle things). And maybe in the major part this will do. And all people in the clan will know about it. Note: the beast, Iconomy likes secrecy. And makes us belief it is good for us too. It created a word to camouflage secrecy: "privacy", it calls it, and makes us very scared of 'risks' when people know things about us. So it can make things endless complicated and not working. It can hide its incompetence in a curtain of smoke and calling for the 'privacy' of its clients. Well if justice worked fine, I should not have to bother about information on me being publicly known, because justice wold take care of my safety. It does not, sometimes on purpose, I feel: "we told you so, think about your privacy...".

So **transparency** is one of the magic keywords. Another thing is we should create -for this thing to be able to work-, again: local social cohesive groups. In which all people know each other and want to live with each other. Probably only this alone would decrease crime figures with lets say 70%. In local communities people are more happy and take a watch over the other, in positive sense: they'll help people in need, and in the sense that they know that a bike parked against a wall belongs to person X, and that person Y fuzzing around with it is a stranger...

Remember what I stated on the Iconomy principle to maximally separate people and even worse: put people next to each other, which don't know each other, and have different habits, tastes, etc. Who probably will not become friends...

And let's simplify things. I was discussing this topic with a girlfriend of mine, Mirjam Nugteren, which I became to knew a great freethinker and somebody with a great practical talent. I said: why not make it completely transparent on the web what somebody did[35]. Respectful. Of course with the

[35] An important thing is that when person X has published untrue data or behaved not respectfully, and this comes out, this fact will be published about X... an

opportunity for the 'offender' to say his thing about it. She than came with the example she read in the book. It was so simple. We both agreed that this simple concept would be say seven times more *effective* than we have nowadays (in terms of preventions and in terms of bringing 'justice'). And it at least is seventy times more *cheap* than the present system. So, why not implement it, and then evaluate and see where the gaps arise?

The example she read came from a book called "Kinderen van Moeder Aarde" [English: Children of Mother Earth], by the Dutch writer Thea Beckman. I don't know whether it has been translated to English. Offenders got a mark on there forehead. Seven categories were defined, depending on the severity of the crime. And the most sever color would remain for seven years on your forehead, minor acts left a dot for one year.

The example is maybe a bit over the edge, but the idea is the same: use transparency as the remedy. I propose to use the web. If we had this mechanism put to action already, the Dutch Joran van der Sloot wouldn't have killed another girl in South America. That land would have checked the global transparency people base and wouldn't have let Joran in. So that girl is also killed by our nowadays failing juridical system.

In the Netherlands the "College Protection Personal information" ([Dutch: College Bescherming Persoonsgegevens] Did a great job: now you can get a fine of 25.000 euro if you show a burglar on the web.

Yeahh, I know why our leaders will say we should not do this: In the Netherlands the 'Raad van State' (the highest organ

---

important task of the eco subdomain Justea to take care of, to guard this.

of steering) if packed with people who practically all studied 'law', were previous judges, or still have connections with the big law firms. They cannot even *see* that this could work, it is behind their comprehension. Like psychiatrists have to commit something like professional suicide to see that the psychiatric system is insane for the larger part, these people have to do that for their practice.

For me, lawyers and judges have been given a great gift. To decide over the faith of people. For me, advocates and the juridical system have abused this gift in a huge manner. And thus do not deserve this position in the new world. The same for eg. bank directors and (many) psychiatrists, getting loads of money, but not aiming for the true well being of the people they should take care for.... and remember: there is always time to change the path you are on, I once too was interim manger at banks... I too once was a mercenary, giving my strength to the wrong system... everybody can change.

Yes, we live in strange times. Renewal times. Times of the big Change. And only for those who have the strength and competence to see the mechanisms, and let go of their own certainties, there is place in the lead to get us out of the ice age approaching us... this takes rational and emotional strength. And a constructive ego...

So in essence the redesign consists of:

- **Transparency** on the web. If the track record of those lying politicians was already on the web, they wouldn't have been in the Parliament. Simple. **Truth finding** without judging is the first 50% of the newly to be developed Justea.
- **Rebuild** the value and law system. Laws may only exist with a clear requirement and owner.
- Have a **chief / hooder** like model instead of lawyers and judges.

- Keep the big **money** out of the justitea system. Preferably people working there only get a base income. The nice thing: within the Flowconomy this is already arranged for...

And probably it is a good idea to build a community of people who find it OK -within that community- that people say things about each others behaviour (positive and negative). We can take a good example on the counchsurfing community portal where people have a trust ability level based on the friendship someone has, his or her track record, etc.

A final note on the name... I feel I want a newly constructed unique term instead of 'Justea' or 'Justice'. Transparency and / or truth finding should be expressed more in the word, as well as prevention and creating a safe society... if someone has suggestions... let me know!

<u>Change proposal</u> after 13 August 2011 Novaglobe symposium: it is felt that the name of the sub domain should express the need for desire explicitly. Therefore the name '**Transjustice**' is proposed. It has the two main elements in it: I. Bring transparency
II, Bring justice (and prevention).

18 Eco subdomain VII - Iciety

The Iciety stands for 'ICT-Society'. It does not stand for second life, in which a virtual reality has been created, where figures often look far different than they do in real. In which the physical world does not count anymore. And in which people start to do the wildest things because they live in a cramped 'real' world.

Thinking about Iciety, think more of social media as Twitter and Facebook. The special thing about Twitter is that when you do not put up your Real face, the real you as an logo (avatar) on your account, people will not like you, and probably un follow you the sooner or later. It is about true-id's, in other words: that someone who says he is person X, he really *is* person X.

I guess the 'College on Protecting Personal Information' in the Netherlands will not like this, they don't like transparency... (see previous chapter).

And that is what the Iciety is about to: when somebody says it is person X, it *is* person X. Only in this way we can build a trusted environment. This trust will bring the people joining this community. Why? It is far more nice to live in a world in which you can trust and see people. Bad people will have a mark, so you can distinguish them. Or they decide not to be in the Iciety, that is their choice.

Within the Iciety goodness and transparency will proof to -even in economical terms- lead to prosperity. In the present society bad conduct is rewarded, within the Iciety this will be good behaviour. As stated in the chapter on 'the revival of the goodness', good networks have the ability to outperform bad networks, if they join forces, and keep the gate closed for bad influences.

But the Iciety goes further than Twitter and Facebook. It is based on a global ICT architecture, on top of the Internet. It is a next level up. A next layer, providing for global functions. And thus providing for the Flowconomy in the digital world.

Within the Iciety you do not need thick contracts and lawyer bills to start a cooperation or do an transaction. Simply because you can *see* that your partner is reliable, and that the basis is a WE-conomy and not a I-conomy. The WE-conomy is based on working together, the Iciety is more like a battlefield, a competition, where you have to cover your back with each step you do.

ICT is the ring of Power. ICT is the enabling factor with which we can realise Novaglobe. Mainly for two reasons:

1. It allows us to connect, and distinguish good people from bad people. And due to transparency everywhere

the classical method of divide and conquer (and keep things secret), which have served first religion, than kings, than 'the Iconomy' subsequently, will not work anymore.

2. It allows us to create a enormous efficient ecology. Each talent and resource is available and can be found. With one or two days work a week we can do, what we do now in five days... The Venus Project -or a sort alike initiative- can be realised.

18.1 Analysis

First, when we look around us, we can notice that ICT within about 20 years has penetrated all ecological functions. An merely has brought goodness. I would say there is especially one sector in which it has brought evil as well: the financial sector.

Within the financial sector ICT has leveraged the already bad things at hand of the creation of money, and creating all kinds of financial products to push profits further and further, and enlarge the debt-balloon. All kinds of financial products like options, swaps, and combinations of all kinds of products would not have taken such a influence without ICT.

And ICT connected all local economies via debt-structures towards each other, making one mega Iconomy which can only collapse as a whole or grow as a whole. Why is it a problem that people in Greece have a lower 'efficiency' ratio than other countries? If they are less 'efficient' for whatever reason (can be just bureaucracy, or corrupt people, or just the 'Mediterranean pace'). The answer: debt.

We collectively created a bomb by tie-ing Greece to the European Union. It has been our own Greed and 'Fattening Syndrome' (see appendix on the Five Syndromes of Mysery Creation). The citizens of Greece don't understand anything of banking nor the financial markets. Our political and bank sector leaders, they are the only ones to blame for this... and even they do not understand the total system dynamics of the financial market. So are they to blame? The Beast, the Iconomy is unleashed... is gotten out of control. And will strike back to the people who created this monster.

In the past, when a country just sort of broke down, it resulted in that its currency would become of less value, and that's it. Nowadays the whole world panics, mainly because they have *interests* in that country. The have lend billions and billions of euro's and thus put a whole country and its citizens in a debt chain. And if the government is not able to pay back those debts, then the whole world has a problem. But wasn't it a bad thing to lend the money in the first place? In islamtic banking lending and interest are bad things. I agree.

But here too, if ICT wasn't there things would have remain loosely coupled.

Some other observations are:

- There is a 'strange' panic on 'privacy', mainly fed by the government. "Watch out not to name your name on the Internet!".
- We have a Internet which does not authenticate its visitors by default.
- Social media have become normal (Facebook, Twitter, etc).
- Even in the 'poorest' countries, everybody seems to get access to the Internet.
- Information which would have took tens of years to reach all people on the world, can do the same in some hours.

So, maybe the Internet even may make the country borders fade. On the Internet country borders do not exist, even countries like China try to take advantage of the web at one end, and trying to block it at the other.

As I stated earlier, when we can created a shared back bone, we can implement global functions: one encyclopedia (Wiki, already exists), one shared operating system (Linux / Ubuntu, already exist). What is next? Can't we implement a currency globally? Can't we implement a justice and peace system globally?

Yes we can.

But the strange thing is: this will 'cost' millions of jobs. And the economists made us believe this is a problem. Why? The same added valued remains being created, so there should be the same value to give to the people (let's call it money).

Or can we conclude that the whole system of giving people jobs is a way to keep them of the street?

Or can we conclude that the present system is not looking for an efficient way of doing things? It think the latter is true. By doing it in this manner some people become extremely rich. And many are poor and have to work very hard for the rich people. That is my conclusion. That is the Iconomy.

18.2 Requirements on the Iciety

Based on the previous described analysis, we come to the following requirements / wishes for the Iciety design:

1. Of course, it should focus on a **global** orientation
2. It should be based on the open source dynamics, which has already manifested itself in the Internet world.
3. It should serve the previous described six main **Novaglobe eco subdomains** maximally, and serve the underlying values in its backbone (see the Goodvalues chapter: transparency, avoid theft, criminality, etc).
4. It should be based on a global **ICT architecture**, providing for basic global functions on which people from all over the world can plug in their own functions. Typical global services could be: a global currency, a global name service (maybe with room for websites, content publishing, your own webshop / services publisher, etc.), a global service for making ones

trustability explicit, a global service for reducing crimes and tracking down criminals, etc.

5. It should be based on **organisational renewal**, meaning that even the basic function implementations can evolve and that somebody stands up and creates an alternative.

18.3 Design

To put things at work in a efficient way, it would be good:

- to have a common social community
- have the global functions implemented
- have functions which provide for trust and transparency

About findability and trust

For thos who want it, it should be good to have some kind of registration for true id's. And unique names, so you can easily find somebody you are looking for.

Platforms like linkedin already provide for this.

Maybe an additional tool 'trustseeker' or something should be created. This tool could analyze graphs of relations and thus giving me an estimation on somebodies trust-ability if I enters his name.

The nice thing is: we do no have to make this obligatory: if you want to be a player in the new world, find customers and business partners, better take care of your Internet profile, find-ability and trust-ability. This mechanism will take care for people to make them selves transparent on the web.

But again, the existing structures / static system does not want or like it. Companies doe not like their employees to be on the web. That is why I think more and more people will not work anymore for a 'company', but are individuals, working in dynamic organisations. The Iciety provides for a platform for this.

18.3.1 Examples on global implementations

18.3.2 A Global (web)store

Nowadays there are several Internet based stores. The most known ones are Ebay for second hand goods, and Amazon for books.

The interesting thing is that they both went to the stock market to get 'required capital' to achieve the required market share. And thus are part of the Iconomy.

But this step also made them expensive: shareholders want money.

What would happen if we make a global sourced store? Based on the Flowconomy underground, and maybe even completely open sourced?

We could use a common service for identification of people, and add a function of top of it 'store'. The identification service is directly connected to the global implemented currency function. So no problems and money leaks (transaction costs) at services as Paypal or credit card companies (it is all facilitated by the open source community).

Furthermore we would ask open source developers to join and make plugins for the global store.

And especially the second hand and 'give away' flow would certainly flourish, because you only have one place to look, and all people having things around which they want to give away or sell put them with a photo and short description at the global-store. Imagine that every little thing produced can be found in such way? And imagine all kinds of smart solutions like intelligent image interpreters which automatically catalog your things. You only make three pictures, and the global-store takes care of the rest.

Imagine we have personal shop pages functionally available, the only thing we have to do is to make a 'global collect' webshop function, which regularly passes all shops and put the information in the global index.

This could boost reuse enormously... note that things can be just given away as well (that ask no money for it).

18.3.3 An intelligent package delivery service

And imagine a global postal and package service? I recall the buses form about five different service companies driving though the peripheries of the place I live. All bringing one letter or package. So many hidden loss to get rid of. Causing so many people hours doing useless things and energy (fuel) being spoiled. It is better to make one organisation do all.

18.3.4 Crowdweb or CrowdWIFI?

imagine each cellphone being a WIFI receiver *and transmitter*. This makes it possible that 1. We don't need a (commercial) WIFI supplier, 2. maybe we can even run our own Internet.... Of course this will only work if enough content is available, but it is possible and thus making the information flow completely free from commercial institutes and governments: no additional costs anymore to be connected and transport information over the web. And it will cost no money anymore to use the telephone (Voice over IP). The only limiting factor: energy.

And many, many, more great things become achievable once we have a cooperative global orientation.

19 Part III - Implementation - Put it to action

19.1 Introduction

This part contains relatively to the other (Analysis, Design) parts few pages. The reason is that I want to dedicate a larger part of this part to the actual manifestation of a global topology: enlist which organisations are doing what, who joins, who you can contact for which information, etc. I hope to see a cooperation between all kinds of movements and already existing initiatives... so much of what we need is already there. And we don't have time to build it up ourselves. This is the age of the synergy. Of ONE.

I am especially enthusiastic about movements such as

- Ervin Laszlo's Worldshift movement (is already widely known, has local chapters). It has already a council structure implemented.
- The Zeitgeist Movement, Established by Peter Joseph. This movement is also widely known and especially strong in creating awareness on why the system is corrupt, in very practical terms.
- The various transition towns, ecotownships and freeplaces (like Ruigoord near Amsterdam and Christiania near Copenhagen). The reason I find these 'mini movements' interesting is that they are already self organised townships. Minihabitats...

But also movements as Avaaz (the world in action), various peace and environmental movements, the Ekosofia project (Netherlands) and the Venus project (USA) I like to mention.

The only thing we have to do is to glue it together...

Why not?

In the coming chapter you can read:

1. How to make people **free** for the worldshift.
2. What I see as the **practical key issues** for making the system / world shift.
3. Things **you** can do.
4. Implementing the **global topology**.

19.2 Making people free for the world shift

As stated earlier: I don't want to be part of the 'Iconomy' anymore. I certainly want to contribute to society, do all kinds of work, do my share. But I certainly don't want to work at banks...

But then, how do I pay for the rent (about 1100 euro's a month)? Should I start working in the supermarket? I now share my apartment with a German girl (I met her via couchsurfing). That lowers the costs a little, but I my financial buffers is dropping fast.

I frequently think: why am I not allowed just to go to the forest and make myself a little home? It is not allowed in the Netherlands, which comes down that you HAVE to pay rent (at least 500 euro's a month) or you have to buy a house (at least 200.000 euro's).

And thus we are bound to the system... we have been made (or better: become) slaves of the system.

I think a just think to do for the government is to allocate a substantial part of the country to people. That people get a peace of land for nothing, yes, really: nothing. But they do not own it, they become guardians of that peace of land. Say at least 2000 square meters. People can make their own house. Can grow some food if they wish, or make a joint agriculture area. If we all would eat the half of the meat we eat nowadays there is land enough, even in the Netherlands (where the much of the fields are used for meat industry).

But... an important note: these people are not dispersed randomly: they will form habitats. Group of people knowing each other, and having a representative. Together they take care that the place has its freedom, but does not become a 'mess' (otherwise they lose their guardianship).

In such way people become free of their burden to be part of the system. If you want *luxury* (a car, new clothes, etc) you do additional work in 'the system', but for you base benefits you don't have to do that.

Why not?

OK, maybe the previous example is a bit over the top. But I am really thinking about starting living in a camper, to detach myself from the Iconomy-burden of a mortgage or rent. Both concepts which will not be there anymore in the Flowconomy. Unreasonable concepts...

A ask the reader the same question as I asked at the Club of Budapest meeting 21 March 2011: we say we want worldshift. We need it. We say we need new leadership. But how can we free all that potential, now working at multinationals, banks, the government... more and more leaders desire to do something really useful... but cannot escape from the system. They are tied via their money need. **How can we help them?**

19.3 Remove the PIC's

I want to bring back in mind that we actually -to my opinion- succeed in the worldshift when we dismantle the Primary Iconomy Constructors:

1. The greater part of 'business' is done in foundations instead of Ltd's. (PIC1)
2. Lending and money creation does not anymore exist. (PIC2)
3. Government has an incentive to decrease instead of increase. (PIC3)

Look over the chapter on Primary Iconomy Constructors if you wish. And via implementing the Flowconomy (see flowconomy chapter) we at least get rid of PIC1 and PIC2. In the same chapter I also already give a practical road map on how we can put in in action. Of course things need elaboration in more detail, but for now I say: first start doing it!

19.4 Things you can do

Be the change you want to see... more true than ever. You are the voice. Imagine what happens when everybody stopped buying new? (a sentence from the lyrics of the Black Eyed Peas). Or when you buy your goods at a store with a foundation as vehicle under it? You make the change happen than...

Some practical ideas:

- Produce and buy '**ecoloco**': eat only food, produced within 25km where you live, or say do this for 80% of your consumption (do not act black-white). Ask food provider for ecoloco indicator.
- Eat only 1 or 2 out of 5 days meat (sea or land animals, no difference). I call this way of living '**vegamagician**'.
- Live **chivi**: don't put others in debt. Don't take debt, even not for a house (mortgage). Do not ask more income than say 4000 euro[36]'s a month (modesty). Do not have for more than say 30.000 euro's worth in 'things' (put the rest in a foundation or so, and remain guardian or give them away) → share things.

19.5 Implement a global Topology

This is the white canvas, the next step for us together to fill in...

I intend in the next edition of this book (probably released at the beginning of 2012), to present results of our efforts to make a global 'topology', together with other movements.

36 the Netherlands treshhold.

This is also a call for your talents and time... if you feel you can and contribute to this creation, please send a and email to contact@novaglobe.org

We are especially looking for social media experts, people who can and want implement eg. a global ning network moderators and country hosts (people how want to be contact person for a certain country). Don't worry, this Is the new age, you don't have to promise anything.

19.6 Changers Song

I'd like to finish with the Changers Song... we can change this world... together.

[You can download the whole Beefree, Befree the System album at www.iwanjka.com → Creation and Inspiration → Music, or via this link]

Changers Song

[Beefree, album 'Befree the System']

And You, you, you say you can't change this world,

I say you can.

And You, you, you say I can't change this world,
I say I can.

We can change this world Together,
Together we really can make it Work

I, can hear the Angels Sing,
Next to Me
I, can hear the Children Say:
"Come on, write that Song!"

We can change this world Together,
Together we can really make it Work

And I, met the Elves in the Forest, in the Night,
And we sang that Song
And Then, then, then, the Women came,
And they said: "Come on, sing that Song"

And You, you, you, you say I can't change this World.
I say... "We can"

20 Appendix The Five Syndromes of Misery Creation

20.1 Introduction

While writing the 'Diagnosis Lifejam' book, I was wondering how it could be that psychiatry and pharmacy had become so twisted, so far of track. The book I wrote had a cure in it for people who had been diagnosed 'heavily depressed' (and in fact the book contains the basis for a redesign of looking at practically all mental illnesses).
And than I wondered why so many people got depresses (about one out of ten). I thought: "I can try to cure people, but maybe society is sick, and I better can help to cure society?". And than I started looking at all kinds of subsystems: of course the banking system I had been working in th middle of for about 10 years. I looked at the subsystem 'justice' with all it thick law books, lawyers and highly paid staff. I looked at politics, religion, etc, etc. There interesting thing is that I saw the same patterns coming back in each subsystem. I call these the 'Syndroms of Misery Creation' (Dutch: Syndromen van Ellendecreatie). Whether I worked for the government to optimise the Dutch harbor processes, or working at the bank... everywhere happened the same.
And... I am 'afraid' the male dominance has an important factor... The song below, by the Dire Straits I already sing for about 20 years... only since about three years I understand the message...

"I have legalised robbery
Called it belief
I have run with the money
I have hid like a thief
I have re-written history
With my armies of my crooks
Invented memories
I did burn all the books"

[The Men's too strong, Dire Straits]

The man has created quite some misery throughout the ages. Religion as we know it is one of the best examples. But the psychiatric Bible (the DSMIV book) has been created by a similar path: started by men (mainly Freud) and than augmented and copied by other men who benefit from to power the book brings to them. Even if the book contains a lot of nonsense or contradictions.

But, let us not talk about guild. Forgive the sinners. And Freud was probably a victim of is own emotion, ego and mental disharmony. And so where all the men who added pieces to the 'holy' writings probably. And maybe without the male 'eagerness' we wouldn't have a computer now, and would have no car. But... I see a brighter world. In which we can release the nonsense and keep the sense...

"The Survival of the fittest has ended,
The Revival of the Goodest has just begun"
[Iwanjka]

I think it is time there comes more space for the emotional-spiritual side, instead of basing our course on the rational and material side only (Iconomy). Let us stop using physical violence. No more repression and abuse of people. No more wars. We can live as one...

The Syndromes of Misery creation describe why it is logical that organisations as big bangs actually became terminal. And why nobody takes action. We miss 'organisational renewal' in our society. This goes for both organisations as jobs. It should be normal that we dismantle organisations after say 30 years of existence. Without letting them go bankrupt. Why? Because within the organisation all kinds of movements take place why it is not vivid, flexible and agile anymore... And people will get more and more like zombies of they not change places...
No more working class hero's. I plead for letting go the 'job for life' contracts.

An example of what happens because of the Five Syndroms of Misery creation. Are you familiar with the 'Peter Principle'? This principle says that each manager gets promoted to his or her level of incompetence. And do you think the managers leaves that position? No... he keeps on sitting there as long as possible and tries to reach his retirement, to guarantee a nice retirement. And when you imagine that each manager manges 25 employees... and that these employees -for instance working at a government- do things 'for' people in the society. Than you can images what kind of thinks the the ordinary people feel themselves confronted with: quite some idiotery. And I am confronted with this at a weekly basis.... Imagine what would happen is those non functioning managers (I think it is at least 80% of the managers) are replaced by functioning managers... in economical terms... I think this would give an efficiency boost of at least 50%.
That is why I plead for that people never stay longer than 3 years at the same position.

I think that when we create an ecology in which the Primary Iconomy Constructors are gone, the most of the Misery Creating Syndroms are gone too, are at least will have far less influence.

20.2 The Five Syndromes of Misery Creation

1.Complication syndrome
[Dutch: Complicatiesyndroom]
People, especially men, have the treat to make things more and more complicated. Take a look at the 'rules'. Take a look at the complexity around the tax system. In the Netherlands you almost need a consultant to fill in your tax forms. And where ICT makes things easier, the tax department takes advantage of this to introduce even more complex rules, because ICT makes this possible...
But take a look as well at the legislation books. It is growing, growing, never gets less. I once read an article by a high positioned lawyer, he said we really should simplify legislation... after him. The extent on injustice grows in the same pace as the

thickness of the law books. "We follow the rules..". But by applying rules, people tend to forget to think (and feel). They are so occupied with administration, reading documents, writing documents, reporting, etc.
People want to make themselves indispensable, so create complex things only they understand (a common practice within ICT, but I think this will go for each domain). And thus safeguarding the organisation needs to hire them for a long, long time, and that their remains enough work.

2. Fattening Syndrome
[Dutch: Uitdijsyndroom]
Things are always becoming more. A department at the government only grows. But the same I saw at banks. Several mechanisms cause this:

1. The manager wants to enlarge his own kingdom. When he 'supervises' more people, it means more prestige, more food for his destructive ego, and a higher salary.
2. People who work at such a department will fill gaps in their work load by creating something new. I saw this happening a lot at the banks I worked for. This feeds the complication syndrome as well, because processes won't get more simple. Even is there is no reason for a new rule, we create a reason...

And who is going to terminate his own job? I only know a few who did so. And I actually only sow free entrepreneurs do this (no one being employed) setting.

3. Control syndrome
[Dutch: Controlesyndroom]
We life in a illusion that if we are controlling more and more, and create mote and more rules, things get better. Forget it. I recently visited Teguize, a small village at Lanzarote (a Spanish island). I spoke with Fred, a Dutch man who started a little cafe-

restaurant there. I consider Lanzarote a relatively free and tolerant area. But bureaucracy and the Misery Creating Syndromes found it as well: Fred told me about an old woman. Who organised a water-fight playing with kids. The police gave her a fine. Everybody happy except for the government staff who felt they had do do something, en thus spoiling the joy of the children and the village.

The control syndrome at work.

And this example is about something I miss in the Netherlands: an adult who goes playing with a group of children of the neighborhood. I haven't seen it happen. Why? We do not dare. And people don't know eachother anymore who live just next doors (see Togetherhood chapter as well). You don't give your child along with somebody you don't know that well, and we are -more than reasonable I feel- scared the child might hurt itself. Again a reason why I believe in the creation of micro and minihabitats...

And in the Netherlands there are so many rules for bars and cafes, it is a wonder they can function at all. I see this as a consequence of too many government-people: all those departments and staff have to do something, so they start to create idiot rules, even often not aligned with other government departments. And the people and entrepreneurs get squeezed in between.

The same goes for the banking sector. About each three years a new set of legislation we had to implement at the bank: Sarbanes Oxley Act, Tabaksblad (Dutch code of conduct), Basel II, etcetera. Thousands of pages of microlegislation. Did dit make the risk taking behaviour at banks better? No, worse. Did it make the bonus ethos at banks better? No, worse. Recently one of the most corrupt banks went bankrupt for lending to much money... society is still recovering from the evil product it sold to its customers (all kind of financial derivate products, without telling the whole story to its customers). And the owner-president? He is now creating a new business... (Primary Iconomy Constructor -

Accountability avoidance).

So creating more rules is exactly the wrong direction. But only when it does not threaten government people to loose their job can make things better, because as long as they stay at their positions, there will remain loads of rules. And this on its turn is related to the Mortgage-Pardon (see Flowconomy, and Frhome type of foundations) and the Flipped Maslow Pyramid.

4. Me-Benefit Syndrome

[Dutch: Geldingsdrangsyndroom]

This syndrome is twofold: it is about the aim for gaining money (like the Primary Iconomy Construct, profit making at business level), and it is phenomenon that people want to 'leave a mark'. Want themselves manifested and heart. Even if it is not good. Within the bank the culture was: the more meetings where scheduled in you agenda the higher your status. Work efficient and do things is such way we don't have to meet? Not important.

I want a world where we are happy with ourselves as we are. And live modest. And like giving without asking something in return... the Givonomy instead of the I-conomy...

5. Fallacy syndrome

[Dutch: Drogsyndroom]

The dutch word drog means fallacy... and is sound like 'drug', interesting. This is the phenomenon that forced by destructive emotions -mostly men- start to make thing up. I think the woman in general is just a bit further in the evolution...

A little side story: I see the evolution layers as a sequence of physical, ration, emotional, soul... Men are strong at the physical layer and rational layer. But not at the emotional layer (and were sense resides). This is illustrated as well when a man and woman enter a conflict: both organisms go tot there comfort zone: the man goes down (physical, starts to use physical violence), the woman goes up (emotional level). For a woman is it far more difficult to use physical violence, she feels it is not good...

And... the men have brought the women often to a position to be able to abuse here (in few rights in the marriage, in prostitution, abuse, etc.). The Bible states that the woman is wrong and guilty. This is not so strange if you take a look at who wrote the Bible. Men?

And the men than makes up a story why it is justified to do so. The church did that, but even in modern society men did that by making prostitution a normal thing, even a by law instituted thing. I believe 90% of the women do not work in this sector by free choice, so are in fact raped by men. Men close their eyes and make up a story it is the women's own desire.

A typical Fallacy Syndrome...

And the DSM IV book and psychiatric theories on mental sicknesses I see as one huge Fallacy Syndrome (but I do not blame people for not seeing it, I have been working 10 years in the banking sector without seeing it is corrupt...). Time comes closer that this 'industry' will see it too, no more obscured by clouds. The DSM V book now adds elements with which Steven Reiss based his work on (The Normal Personality). Soon it will proof it is the only reasonable way, and it will proof psychiatry has been on a long, long side trip... and hopefully finding the just trail soon... more on this in the 'Diagnosis Lifejam' book I wrote.

21 Appendix: Books forming the basis of the quantum leap upwards

Books I advice to read:

Title, author	Why?
2012 the Chaos Point, Ervin Laszlo	Ervin Laszlo has been active in the field of ecology for many years. He even joined the Club of Rome once. And he established the Club of Budapest. In this book he makes very plausible that all kinds of diverging trends

	(climate, finance, etc.) come together around 2012. And he makes clear that this 'Chaos Point' will be followed by a quantum leap upwards or downwards. But that we, the people, should not sit and stare. But create the platform for the quantum leap upwards. And this will be a system shift. Therefore this books fits ultimately with the idea of Novaglobe on redesigning the system and start migrating. Ervin also established www.worldshiftnetwork.org. This book forms a generic basis for all **eco subdomains**.
Equality Freedom Conectivity[37], Martijn Brasem	Martijn has been working for years in development of cities and habitats, as an architect. He describes via his own way why the present system is not good, and he poses practical, directly implementable instruments to make this world a better place. Martijn nowadays works as one of the creators of Ekosofia, a small ecological township near Amsterdam. This book forms a generic basis for all **eco subdomains**.
New Netherland, Jan Frank Koers	Jan Frank founded the political party New Netherlands. One of his studies is economics. In this book he describes a plan for 'Netherland 2.0'. Items such a circulation money and a base income for all are covered. As well as a thorough simplification of the administrative government processes. Note: the ideas in the Novaglobe are more about a 'Netherland 7.0'. The fundament under the books of Jan Frank and Iwanjka are the same however. This book forms a generic basis for all **eco subdomains**.
A History of God, Karen Armstrong	This book inspired me for synthesizing the Goodvalues. And the idea that all religions actually made an icon of God (trespassing Mozes's words). Maybe we should not name 'god', and just call our belief 'Thing' or something like that. This book is a solid base for the sense giving part (which is allocated to the **Artscience** subdomain).
Destructive Emotion and How to Heal them, Daniel	This book gives a strong insight in how we can replace destructive emotions into constructive emotions. Therefore I see the book as relevant for the construction of the **Togetherhood** and **Humansound**

[37] This book is only available in Dutch at this moment, Dutch title: 'Gelijkheid Vrijheid Verbondenheid' publisher, Deniesa. Available via www.boekenroute.nl.

Goleman (in dialogue met the Dalai Lama).	subdomains.
The Normal Personality, Steven Reiss	Steven Reiss is a American professor in psychology. He has written a book which make plausible DSM IV (and V) is pretty useless. A sound base for the **Humansound** subdomain.
Diagnosis Lifejam[38] (only available in the Netherlands, "Diagnose Levensklem")	Based on his own experiences Iwanjka Geerdink describes his process of getting jammed in life, getting seven psychiatric diagnosis in half year time and his way out. Based on the works of Steven Reiss an alternative methode for curing depression is posed: the 'RdRemedy'. The book is a basis for constructing a new mental care system within the **Humansound** subdomain.
The Whole Elephant, Marja de Vries	A solid basis for understanding the relation between quantum mechanics, goodness, pyramids, religion, law of attraction and our bodies. An important base for the **Humansound** and **Artscience** subdomain. See this link.

And watch Zeitgeist Moving Forward, download www.zeitgeistmovie.com

As you can see, not all eco subdomains are covered yet. If you know about books specific for a subdomain, or want to write one, please contact me, and maybe I can enlist that book here. Email: iwanjka@novaglobe.org

<u>Imagine</u>

Imagine there's no Heaven
It's easy if you try
No hell below us
Above us only sky
Imagine all the people
Living for today

Imagine there's no countries

38 This book is only available in Dutch at this moment, Dutch title: "Diagnose Levenskem", publisher Deniesa. Available via www.boekenroute.nl

It isn't hard to do
Nothing to kill or die for
And no religion too
Imagine all the people
Living life in peace

You may say that I'm a dreamer
But I'm not the only one
I hope someday you'll join us
And the world will be as one

Imagine no possessions
I wonder if you can
No need for greed or hunger
A brotherhood of man
Imagine all the people
Sharing all the world

You may say that I'm a dreamer
But I'm not the only one
I hope someday you'll join us
And the world will live as one

07796291100

9 789081 577540